Ted Engstrom has always inspired me, from age 25 to 65, and now he's done it again and is waiting to do it for you. Oh, I just love the man and his indomitable, irrepressible spirit that so pervades these many inspirational stories of kindred spirits who, like Ted, have walked the talk of filling their senior years with passion, purpose, and service. Years ago, Ted taught me to pray, "Lord, may I finish better than I started." Now in this book, Ted is showing me how. You may be 86, Ted, but thanks, Young Guy!

Michael Cassidy, President, African Enterprise

Ted Engstrom is one of the outstanding evangelical leaders of his generation. As he has entered the ninth decade of his remarkable life, he continues to model in word and deed his passion and purpose for life!

Dr. Paul Cedar, Chairman, The Mission America Coalition

Who is better prepared to write about adding life to your years than Ted Engstrom? Ted is the personification of that himself. And in these personal vignettes he gives example after example, proving that one's sunset years need not be wasted in some combination of indulgence and self-pity. Instead, they can be generative to others, fulfilling for oneself, and productive for the Lord.

John Huffman, Senior Pastor, St. Andrews Presbyterian Church, Newport Beach, CA

Ted Engstrom has been my mentor and example for a lifetime. It began when he was my boss in Youth for Christ and he continued to go before me "making the crooked places straight." Now as I have joined the AARP crowd, I find he is still providing inspiration and example. *Add Life to Your Years: Aging with Passion and Purpose* is a wonderful encouragement to all of us to remain productive. In his usual fashion, this is practical, relevant, solid, Christ-centered, biblical advice. You'll find this book a blessing!

Dr. Jay Kesler, Chancellor, Taylor University, Upland, IN

As a *senior adult,* the apostle John experienced one of the high points of his life's purpose when he received the vision that became the book of Revelation. So Ted Engstrom provides multiple examples of optimum fulfillment of seniors through real-life stories, sage advice, and current resource contacts. *Add Life to Your Years* is a "must read" for everyone in the second half of life. Each chapter reminds us of the unparalleled value and potential of our senior-adult season of life.

Dr. Gordon E. Kirk, Senior Pastor, Lake Avenue Church, Pasadena, CA

Ted Engstrom's go-for-it spirit has been obvious for a long time. When I first knew him as his pastor, Ted was in his mid-forties— with a limp and constant pain (from World War II), but with productivity in every area he touched, a mad schedule, and a bright smile.

As is the man, so is his book. Seniors in pain or otherwise, as you read these "senior stories," let God touch you, motivate you, and use you as never before.

Ray Ortlund, Renewal Ministries

If Moses or the apostle John had retired at 65, we wouldn't have the Ten Commandments or the book of Revelation, and the Jews would never have reached the Promised Land. Ted Engstrom is a remarkable man who has been a friend to almost every Christian ministry leader since World War II. By his own example, and now through this inspiring book, Ted debunks the American myth that somehow moving to the Sunbelt and filling our lives with golf, tennis, and leisure is God's highest aspiration for our senior years. At 86, Ted Engstrom is still as passionate about ministry as he was at 36. He is one of my heroes and has set a standard for all of us to aspire to.

Rich Stearns, President, World Vision United States

Add *Life* to Your Years

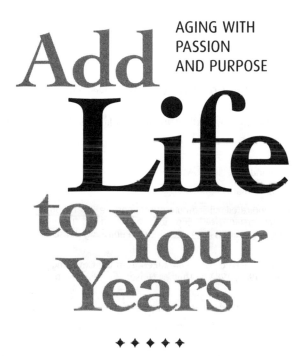

Add Life to Your Years

AGING WITH PASSION AND PURPOSE

✦✦✦✦✦

TED W. ENGSTROM
with Joy P. Gage

Tyndale House Publishers, Inc.
WHEATON, ILLINOIS

Library of Congress Cataloging-in-Publication Data

Engstrom, Theodore Wilhelm, date .
    Add life to your years : aging with passion and purpose / Ted W. Engstrom, with Joy P. Gage.
        p. cm.
ISBN 0-8423-5749-1 (pbk.)
1. Christian aged—Religious life. I. Gage, Joy P. II. Title.
BV4580 .E54 2002
248.8′5—dc21   2001007084

Printed in the United States of America

05 04 03 02
6   5   4   3   2   1

To my fellow residents
at the lovely
Royal Oaks Manor

CONTENTS

FOREWORD

What do you visualize when you hear the term "the golden years"? You probably picture people who are retired—perhaps playing golf with friends or baking cookies for grandchildren. Or you may imagine the Whistler's Mother stereotype: someone sitting in a rocking chair, doing nothing—except growing older and more decrepit by the minute.

But is this really how God intended us to spend our later years? Is retirement as most Americans practice it even a Christian concept?

In my book *How Now Shall We Live?* I describe a common scene near my own home. My wife and I live in an area of Florida that, a few years ago, began attracting upscale retirees: presidents of auto companies, comptrollers of major corporations, and high-powered barons of Wall Street, who settle into their luxurious gated communities surrounded by manicured golf courses, fine restaurants, and swaying palms. They enjoy the American dream come true: no worries, no work, and golf every day.

Many of them follow a predictable pattern—like a man I'll call Charlie. Freed from the pressures of work, Charlie eagerly trots off to the golf course every morning, ends up on the nineteenth hole for a few relaxing drinks, and then arrives home in time to scan the *Wall Street Journal* and take a short nap. At five o'clock Charlie gets out his chartreuse sports jacket with matching checked pants, part of a new wardrobe he purchased at a pricey local men's shop. No more navy pinstripes for Charlie. Then it's off to the club for a cocktail party thrown by his neighbors (we'll call them the Hewitts).

Different neighbors host the party each night, either at their home or at the club. After six weeks or so, the cycle comes back to the Hewitts, and around they go again.

After a cycle or two, Charlie begins to detect a certain sameness to the conversation. People grumble about taxes, share tidbits about the new neighbors, complain about the yard workers or the plumber, compare their grand edifices . . . and, of course, comment on the weather.

"It's a good one today, eh, Charlie?"

"Oh, yeah, but getting muggy."

Charlie even finds his enthusiasm for golf waning somewhat, which is strange because he's loved golf all his life. And he finds that when he skims the *Wall Street Journal*, he sometimes experiences a wave of nostalgia for the good old days when he *had* to read it—and when it often quoted him. He misses striding into the office every morning to begin a new day.

It's usually only six months, a year at the most, before the disillusionment sets in. Charlie is no longer interested in talking about books or current events; the banal cocktail chatter has hollowed out his brain. Besides, he's drinking too much, and his memory is slipping. He's short-tempered and easily angered, particularly by incompetent plumbers and yard workers. When someone swings open a car door recklessly and dings his new Mercedes, he gets really depressed. He begins to wonder how many golf games he has left before he dies. In fact, thoughts like that begin to wake him up in the middle of the night.

Sadly, I know a lot of Charlies—once vital, productive people who have deteriorated into heavy-drinking bores. They long for a sense of fulfillment and dignity that no amount of pleasure can provide.

The fact is, men and women cannot live without purpose. The *Westminster Shorter Catechism* asks: "What is the chief end of man?"

The answer is: "To glorify God and enjoy Him forever."

It's a staggering thought that we can know and glorify and enjoy the sovereign God, fulfilling His purpose through our lives. This all-consuming purpose gives life meaning and direction in all circumstances.

Add Life to Your Years is designed to help those in the later years of life to live a purposeful and passionate life and to finish strong—as the Lord petitions us. The call to serve the Lord echoes throughout life, including the later years. As an older adult, one can still pursue personal growth, challenge oneself to achieve high goals, and live in the light of God's grace.

In this collection of stories, readers will find encouragement to embrace activities that bring joy to others—and fulfillment to the doer. You'll discover inspiring role models, from retired doctors working in the developing world to octogenarians contributing to building churches; from retired teachers mentoring children to retired actors ministering to tourists. You'll find tender stories of those who balance the care of a disabled spouse with daily work toward new life goals.

This book is a reminder that when we retire from our "official" jobs, we should throw our imaginations wide open. Should we continue to use our professional skills in a new way? Or should we develop that lifelong skill we never before had time for?

Readers will learn the key ingredients for staying active throughout life, regardless of physical or financial limitations. A generation of older Americans will learn to uncover their mission and purpose in this important season of life.

For many seniors, the golden years are time to get involved in volunteer work. Through twenty-seven years working in prisons, I have seen thousands of volunteers accept the challenge of working behind prison gates—a tremendously needy mission field here at home. At first volunteers are apprehensive. But once they discover the joy of volunteering, they are new people. They volunteer to bless others, but they're the ones who get blessed.

Ted Engstrom is one of the greatest Christian leaders of our time, one who has inspired and encouraged me repeatedly through my years as a Christian. He has a wonderful attitude about life—and it comes through in these pages. He has lived the faith all of his life and continues to do so today. I'm not surprised that in his later years we find him showing fellow seniors how to make the most of the time left to them. One of my colleagues, looking over the proofs of this book, was so inspired by the stories collected here that she immediately determined to buy a copy for her own parents—retired people who too often do not know how to fill their time.

Like Ted, I don't believe retirement is a biblical concept. Think of older biblical characters: We find them performing purposeful work until the day they die.

I've known many modern seniors who take after them. Even those in failing health never stop looking for ways to serve the kingdom. For instance, many seniors become pen pals with prison inmates—writing letters to offenders that profoundly change their lives. I think in particular of a remarkable woman named Myrtie Howell.

I first heard about Myrtie from an inmate in a New Hampshire prison when he wrote to ask those of us at Prison Fellowship headquarters to join in prayer for her health. Prison Fellowship had matched up this man and Mrs. Howell as pen pals, something we do with thousands of inmates and volunteers.

"Please pray for Grandma Howell," he pleaded in his childlike scrawl, " 'cause she's sick and may be going to die. Nobody has ever loved me like she has. I just wait for her letters; they mean so much."

Our staff began praying for Mrs. Howell. Then some months later I received a letter from the woman herself— reporting on the inmates she was corresponding with and telling me how each one was doing, about their morale and their problems.

She concluded, "Writing to inmates has filled my last days with joy."

Over the next year, Myrtie's letters kept coming always upbeat. In each letter she reported on "her boys" and frequently asked for more names to add to her correspondence list. At one point we tallied that she was actually writing to seventeen inmates. No small task for a ninety-one-year-old woman.

No small task for anyone, for just the thought of writing to prisoners scares most people, including Christians, half to death. They have visions of dangerous criminals getting their names and addresses and, once out of prison, tracking them down for nefarious purposes. Why was this elderly, obviously frail woman different?

I got my answer when a Prison Fellowship seminar was scheduled for the town Myrtie lived in: Columbus, Georgia. I knew I had to make time to meet this woman whose letters could call forth such concern from incarcerated men she had never met.

When I tracked her down, I found that Myrtie lived in an old soot-covered brick high-rise in downtown Columbus, an apartment building converted a few years earlier into a home for the aged.

I rode the elevator to Myrtie's floor and knocked at her door. "Come in, come in," a firm, strong voice shouted.

As I opened the unlocked door, I was greeted by a broad, welcoming smile as Myrtie leaned back in her chair in pleasure, her white fleecy hair neatly parted at the side. We visited for a few minutes, and I started to thank her for her faithful ministry. But before I could finish my first sentence, Myrtie cut me off.

"Oh, no, you've helped me. These last years have been the most fulfilling of my whole life. I thank you—and most of all I thank Jesus."

And I knew that Myrtie, despite living alone in this dreary place, crippled and in continuous pain, really did mean what she said.

The fact is, God isn't going to give us a gold watch, throw us a retirement party, and put us out to pasture—or in a rocking chair. No matter what our age or health, He expects us to continue to use the abilities He has given us—even if all we have the strength to do is pray for others.

Whether we move to Budapest to work with a Christian school, stay close to home to care for grandchildren, or write letters to prisoners, we must never forget for whom it is we are ultimately laboring: the One who called us to reflect His creative activity through our own creativity—the Lord Jesus Christ. When we carry out our work in obedience to God's commands, as Martin Luther reminds us, then God Himself works through us to His purposes.

INTRODUCTION

A number of years ago I wrote a book entitled *Welcome to the Rest of Your Life* (Zondervan). The book dealt with planning for the retirement years. My purpose was to help individuals who were thinking and praying about how they should prepare for a change of lifestyle as senior citizens.

Since that time, Dorothy and I have moved into a very fine retirement center. Prior to our move, we applied the principles that I articulated in the earlier book, and we felt well prepared for the change. We have thoroughly enjoyed these past three years. We have met many committed Christians among the residents who have become very special friends. However, one thing has concerned me deeply. I have sensed that some of these fellow Christian residents live passionless lives. They move from one meal to the next, one day to the next, one month to the next, exhibiting very little purpose. This has troubled me increasingly.

I began to feel a new burden to address senior citizens who love the Lord but appear to lack passion and purpose. Thus this book, the goal of which is to encourage followers of Christ to recognize how meaningful their lives can be in later years.

In order to meet that goal, we have sought to find

people who continue to maintain passion and purpose in their lives well beyond the accepted age of retirement. This book is a collection of their stories.

These are people who, like myself, do not believe that retirement is a biblical concept. (I am eighty-six years old and am not retired; I am on my fourth career.) You will read about doctors in post-retirement years finding time to work in Third World countries; teachers volunteering their services to instruct overseas missionary children; octogenarians contributing many hours to the work of their local churches; seniors taking on caregiving respon- sibilities while maintaining a balanced life; seniors with physical limitations ministering through prayer and note writing. These are people from all walks of life, but they have this in common: They are maintaining purpose and passion in their lives. They would all agree with Douglas Elwood (see page 123), who says, "We should be stewards for a lifetime, not just for two-thirds of our life."

One close friend I had hoped to include in the book led the kind of life I think we as seniors should pursue. At ninety-three years of age, Armin Gesswein continued to conduct his Revival Prayer Fellowship gatherings. He didn't believe in retirement. Once when a well-known minister was introduced to Armin, he said, "Oh, yes. You are retired down here in the South." Armin replied, "That's heresy!" And it was, for he never retired. When first approached about an interview for this book, he regretfully declined because he was scheduled to be in Norway conducting a Revival Prayer Fellowship gather- ing. He consented to schedule a later interview. But Armin went on to his heavenly home before the inter- view could take place.

I am convinced that God has a purpose for each of us that He can reveal by His Holy Spirit as we seek to make these sunset years productive and meaningful. There may be great variety in the tasks He puts before us, but as seniors we share this common goal: to live fruitful lives for the glory of God until we draw our last breath.

✦ ✦ ✦ ✦ ✦

PART ONE

FOREVER GROWING

*It has been said that people grow old by deserting their ideals.
Or in the words of a classic quotation usually attributed to
Samuel Ullman, "Years wrinkle the skin, but to give up
enthusiasm wrinkles the soul."*

*In the following stories you will meet people who are still
pursuing their ideals and who are living their lives with
enthusiasm. Their health varies from trim and fit to fragile and
fighting, but all are reaching toward goals that challenge them.*

*They actively pursue sports or hobbies or new learning
opportunities. They keep abreast of society, write in a journal,
readjust priorities, and make new plans.*

*While all are conscientiously seeking to serve God, their stories
have been included because they represent a select group of
Christian seniors who are forever growing.*

CHAPTER **1**

✦The Renaissance Man

*T*HOSE who know Ed Hayes best call him a
Renaissance man. For decades he has passionately pursued
a variety of interests. He wears many hats: artist, writer,
botanist, world traveler, educator. An ordained minister,
he spent much of his career teaching at the college and
seminary level. He ended his formal working years with
a stint as president of Denver Seminary. Somewhere in
between he put in thirteen years as director of a large
Christian conference center, a move that caused many
to think Ed had "lost his marbles." But he says of the
experience, "I learned something there—that people's
expectations should not control who you are or what you
do in ministry." While at the conference center, Hayes
broadened his knowledge of botany, an interest he still
actively pursues.

With his love for variety, it is only natural that my
friend Ed's senior years should be brimming with diverse
activities. A published author, he admits that though he
likes to write, it is not a passion with him. He confesses to
three great passions: art, botany, and travel. Friends would
add that Ed, along with his wife, Marilyn, demonstrates a
fourth passion—hospitality.

After his formal career ended, Ed and Marilyn bought a

You must have interests. People who come to retirement often are surprised by it and bored by it. If you restrict yourself to what your job defined for you, you are ready for a crash.

ED HAYES

home in Santa Barbara, a modest Spanish-style two-bedroom house with ample space for entertaining weekend guests. Saturday breakfasts are served in the kitchen nook with its interesting array of antiques. Stretching across the top of the cabinets is a row of wooden potato mashers sufficient to prepare an army's daily quota of spuds. Ed and Marilyn prepare the meal together, laying out an inviting table: muffins hot from the oven, fresh fruit in season, juice, a frittata, Marilyn's Swedish coffee, and some exotic blooms from Ed's garden.

In the living room a collection of leather-bound sketchbooks lies on the coffee table. Sketching his way across Europe, Ed has created these elegant travel journals to be handed down to his grandchildren. He has long concentrated on sketching because he believes drawing is the basis of all art. His interest in art began in high school, where his achievements earned him a scholarship to art school. But even then, he was beginning to develop many interests, so he turned down the scholarship and elected to pursue a broader education. He continued to develop his artistic skills on his own by studying the great masters and visiting major art galleries.

In much the same way, Ed developed his interest in botany. He took only one course in botany but has built on that with a lifetime of study. Living in Santa Barbara has allowed Ed to pursue his passion for plants. In nearby

Montecito, his niece, Virginia Hayes, serves as plant curator for the world-class Lotus Land gardens. Ed volunteers as a docent at the gardens, having completed an extensive training course required of all volunteers. Unless they are traveling, Ed will be at Lotus Land conducting a tour from one to three times every week.

Travel is a passion that Ed and Marilyn pursue together. They have set several specific goals: They plan to take each of their six grandchildren to Washington, D.C.; they have a list of major art galleries yet to be visited; they want to visit the birthplace or library of every U.S. president. Marilyn spearheads the last goal, doing all the research and making arrangements. But it is Ed's family connection to President Rutherford B. Hayes that sparked the interest.

Ed believes that the key to enjoying the senior years is to develop more than one interest. He expresses concern for people in academia who come to the close of their teaching years and have no other interests. In the manner of a true Renaissance man, he says, "If I had three lives to live, they would all be for Christ but they would be in some [different] field. I don't want to be poured into a mold. I want to learn something new."

CHAPTER 2

✦Around the World and Going Again

*T*ALL, willowy Donna Thomas surveyed the crowded Beijing street. Everywhere she looked she saw Chinese people uniformly clothed in blue Mao jackets and matching pants. They stopped to stare at Donna, a strange-looking foreigner. She towered above them. Her eyes were shaped differently. Her skin was white. Her hair was brown and curly. She wore Western clothes. And she led a small group of people who looked and dressed just like her.

For sixteen years prior to her trip to China, Donna and her husband had escorted Christian tourists "with a mission" to various places in the Western Hemisphere. Through their organization, Project Partner with Christ, more than four thousand people were exposed to missionary endeavors in Central America, the Caribbean, and South America. Then, as China began to open up to visitors, Donna decided to take a group to Beijing. It proved to be a life-changing decision for Donna—a woman who even then was forever growing.

A peek into Donna's past provides proof that growing almost always requires leaving your comfort zone to meet the challenge of the unknown. She and her husband were happily ministering in a church they founded in Wichita,

If you see where people are hurting, or even where they are happy, you can relate to people and help them. You don't have to be doing all the things that I'm doing. Just see the world through the eyes of Jesus Christ.

DONNA THOMAS

Kansas, when a visiting evangelist challenged them to visit Mexico. Prior to that first Rio Grande crossing, the Thomases had no vital interest in missions. Afterward they founded Project Partner for Christ for the purpose of taking Christian laypeople on vision/work trips to foreign countries.

Donna describes their visit to Mexico as a chance to see the people through Jesus' eyes—the first of many life-changing experiences that promoted growth in Donna's life. In Beijing she caught a glimpse of her faith through the eyes of their assigned bus driver when he posed two separate questions. The first shocked her; the second challenged her thinking. Upon hearing that Donna's group was a Christian group, the bus driver asked, "Is that a religion?" Later, after attending the only Protestant church in Beijing with them, the driver asked Donna, "Does your religion help you with your problems?" Haunted by the question, she was challenged to a new level of spiritual growth—one that would help her with practical problems.

Resolving practical problems often meant moving into the previously unknown. From Mexico to China and beyond, Donna faced a series of faith-enhancing challenges that she describes as climbing one mountain after another. Along the way she became a travel guide, a pilot, a fundraiser, a CEO, and an author. When faced with new responsibilities she accepted the challenge to acquire the necessary training. In the early years of the Thomases' organization, Donna attended meetings sponsored by World Vision for leaders of small missions organizations. She was the only woman among a dozen or more men, and she always had more questions than anyone.

Donna has a theory about forever growing. She believes that people who see the world through Jesus' eyes are the ones who continue to grow. For Donna, seeing the world through Jesus' eyes has kept her open to change, a prerequisite for continual growth. She experienced a big change when her husband died and she moved in as head of the company they founded. This is when I first met Donna. Recently she faced an even more drastic change as she stepped aside, turned over the helm to a young successor, and severed her official relationship with the company. "It was time," she said. Donna is living proof that recognizing when to take the next step is as important to growth as recognizing what that step will be.

Now in her seventies, she is still traveling around the world as a consultant for missions projects. These days she is apt to have one or more of her grandchildren with her. Her goal is to take each one to a foreign country—a great growth opportunity that she believes is worth a year of college education.

Change remains a part of Donna's life as she moves into her latest challenge—to promote her book, *Climb Another Mountain*. It gives her an opportunity to tell audiences what her friends already know: So long as Donna Thomas draws a breath she will be looking for new challenges, searching for that next mountain to climb. She will be forever growing.

CHAPTER **3**

✦Goal: To Live
until I Die

*V*ISITORS to the Gillikin home in San Carlos,
California, must exit a quiet, steeply winding street to
reach the redwood condominium complex where Bob
and Betty make their home.

Approach to their ground-level residence is by means
of a redwood deck that ends at the front door through
which, on any given day, one is apt to hear strains of a
piano: scales, show tunes, gospel music, or Beethoven.
Especially Beethoven. Betty, now in her early seventies,
practices forty-five minutes per day, and this year she is
perfecting Beethoven's Sonata op. 7.

While it may not be unusual for a seventy-two-year-old
woman to keep up with her piano skills, for Betty
Gillikin, the discipline represents an ongoing goal to
continue growing so long as she has life.

Over fourteen years ago doctors told Betty that at most
she had three years to live. For four and a half years the
debilitating pain of a rare disease left her unable to play
the piano.

Before she was diagnosed, Betty endured a lengthy
series of tests. Her primary physician was the first to voice
his suspicion that Betty had *scleroderma,* a fatal illness. (It
was later determined that she also had a second equally

SAGE ADVICE

✦✦✦✦✦

*D*on't give up. Don't say, "I can't handle it," because you *have* to handle it. The way I handle it determines how Bob feels, because if I'm just griping about everything, he's not happy either. Illness doesn't give us any excuse to gripe.

BETTY GILLIKIN

rare, fatal disease.) As she awaited the official diagnosis, Betty made a decision: Whatever time she had left, she would make it her goal *to live until she died.*

The Gillikins faced their future by determining that if they had only one more year together, they would make it the best possible year.

In the beginning, managing the pain and the effects of Betty's disease demanded a lot of time and attention. While unable to offer a cure, doctors did find ways to treat the symptoms. Gradually the Gillikins established new routines to accommodate the lifestyle that had become their lot.

Bob has continued in his position as senior associate pastor of the seven hundred-member church where he has served for seventeen years. Because the church facilities are located near their home, he is readily available for any emergency Betty might face. If necessary he can stop in at noon, fix lunch for her, and walk Nellie, their sheltie dog. Although his church-related responsibilities are heavy, he has made one major concession to Betty's illness: He has eliminated most of his evening meetings, thus allowing him to spend after-dinner hours with Betty.

During the day, to lessen pain and stress to her legs, Betty sits with them propped in front of her on the sectional sofa. Through large picture windows at the back

12

of their house, she has an excellent view of the surrounding hills and the valley in between. Deer can often be seen feeding among the redwoods. In this pleasant surrounding Betty reads, journals, prays, and keeps in touch with friends via the telephone. With careful management of her energy she is able to do household tasks and take her sheltie companion for short walks.

Enjoying life one day at a time has been easier since the Gillikins learned to plan Bob's off days more carefully. If there are pressing errands, they make an outing of it. Betty goes along in her wheelchair to the local supermarket while Bob does the actual shopping. If there are no errands, they often go to the nearby bay, where paved walkways allow Bob to push Betty along in her chair.

Extended trips have proved impractical, but the Gillikins continue to get away together for minivacations. Through the generosity of a friend they enjoy periodic three-day retreats at Pajaro Dunes, a pleasant one-hour drive from their home. Sometimes they take another couple along, thus providing needed social contact that could easily be neglected in their current circumstances.

Betty admits that coming to terms with inactivity has been a big hurdle for her. She spent many years discipling women and conducting Bible studies. Now, as with many who are shut in because of illness, she wonders whether she has a ministry left. But Bob is quick to point out that Betty is having a far-reaching ministry through modeling how to handle chronic illness.

He explains, "It's amazing to see so many people come up to me and say, 'You don't know what it does for me to watch Betty handle this difficulty.' In some respects she is having a more effective ministry now than when she was doing all kinds of things. I think many times we are having our best ministry when we don't even know we are ministering."

Betty acknowledges that there have been blessings as well as hurdles. Although she suffered periodic bouts of depression throughout her life, she points to the fact that she has not had a single episode since the onset of her disease.

Doctors make no attempt to explain Betty's fifteen-year survival record. Nor do the Gillikins make any conjectures about the future. Their daily prayer is not so much, "Add years to Betty's life" as it is "Add life to Betty's years."

With "to live until I die" as her ongoing goal, Betty continues to live one day at a time. And for now, living one day at a time includes spending part of the day perfecting Beethoven.

"Beethoven is like chocolate," Betty says. "Therapeutic."

CHAPTER 4

✦ Still Winning
on the Courts

*J*ACQUE and Larry Campbell have filled a bookcase, a china cabinet, and a wall or two in their Arizona home with medals and trophies captured in tennis tournaments. A dining-room display features a framed picture of the couple surrounded by gold and silver medals. Jacque, a petite, athletic-looking woman in her seventies, sits at the dining-room table, a scrapbook open before her. She sports an engaging grin as she recalls the excitement of marching with ten thousand athletes in the Summer Games. It was the same year she captured a bronze medal in the tennis doubles competition. Larry, the quieter of the two, looks on. Tall, trim, and fit-looking, he appears younger than his eighty-five years.

Sitting across from the Campbells, one might think that Jacque is reminiscing about the distant past and that the Campbell medal collection is from the couple's younger days. The truth is, this husband and wife duo is still winning on the courts. The Campbells are part of the fastest growing athletic movement in the country, the Senior Olympics.

The Senior Olympics Summer Games began in 1987 with 2,500 athletes. A dozen years later, 12,000 participated in 16,000 entries in the 18 sports offered. Also

STILL WINNING ON THE COURTS

♦♦♦♦♦

We seniors should pay attention to our health needs. Make keeping physically fit a priority. People tell me they wish they could do what Larry and I do. But you have to take the first step. Get started.

JACQUE CAMPBELL

known as the Summer National Senior Games, the Senior Olympics is now one of the largest multisport events in the world. As an organization, the National Senior Games Association devotes much time and effort to the support of fitness programs for seniors.

Currently the Senior Games movement involves more than 250,000 seniors.

The Campbells admit that their enthusiasm for tennis started late in life. They began to take it seriously at an age when most people are thinking about giving up the game.

"I was too busy [in my younger years] raising quarter horses and playing softball and volleyball," Jacque explains. "I thought that tennis was a sissy game. I certainly found out differently when I began to play."

Serious about their game, the Campbells take lessons from a tennis pro and, in spite of the more than hundred-degree Mesa summers, they play almost year-round. Between court days, they keep in shape by exercising and walking their dogs.

They are very active with leagues and tournaments at local, state, and national levels. The Senior Olympics requires contestants to qualify through winning at lower levels. In order to enter a national competition, athletes must first win a gold or silver medal in state competition. Both Larry and Jacque have qualified for the national games on numerous occasions.

In addition to participating in the Senior Olympics, the Campbells enjoy swinging their racquets against contestants from around the world in the Huntsman World Senior Games. Although athletes need not qualify to enter the Huntsman Games, the competition is no less formidable. Whether in the Senior Olympics or in the Huntsman World Senior Games, the Campbells play according to age division. Between them they have brought home four gold medals, two bronze medals, and numerous first-place prizes.

The opening ceremonies of the Senior Olympic Summer Games is patterned after the "real Olympics" with the carrying of the torch, the lighting of the flame, and a mass march of competing athletes. While it all adds to the excitement of the event, Jacque Campbell enthusiastically points out that the biggest thrill is marching with ten thousand other athletes who range in age from fifty to ninety.

Larry and Jacque each came to Christ as adults. "So it was pretty special for us," she explains. "It certainly gave our lives a new direction." For many years they were active in the music area of the church. But unlike their bodies, their voices have not fared so well with age. Their main involvement now is with Bible study and prayer groups. Their involvement with tennis provides a potential opportunity for helping others with spiritual needs.

Keeping fit, spiritually and physically, helps the Campbells maintain purpose in their lives. According to Jacque, their athletic endeavors leave them feeling better, looking better, and experiencing better health. "Look at Larry," she says. "You would never know he is eighty-five years old."

Contacts:

The National Senior Games (The Senior Olympics)
National Senior Games Association
3032 Old Forge Drive
Baton Rouge, LA 70808
(225) 925-5678
Fax: (225) 216-7552
www.nationalseniorgames.org

The Huntsman World Games
For information on these games, contact:
St. George Area Convention and Visitors Bureau
1835 Convention Center Drive
St. George, UT 84790

The United States Tennis Association, Inc.
707 Alexander Road
Princeton, NJ 08540
(609) 452-2580
Fax: (609) 452-2265

CHAPTER **5**

✦Making Sure the Music Never Stops

*A*LWAYS GROWING is the goal that keeps musicians Roy and Phyllis Deffinbaugh going . . . and going . . . and going. Between Elderhostel music programs, summer masters programs for musicians, performance schedules, and keeping up with friends, the Deffinbaughs see a lot of road time.

The two former schoolteachers look at music as a gift you can give to people all your life, especially if you continue to hone your skills. Roy plays trombone. Phyllis plays piano. Neither majored in music, but each started playing in fifth grade and never stopped. In recent years Phyllis has begun taking lessons again. Roy studies on his own by listening to the compact discs of his favorite musicians. One such artist plays with the San Francisco symphony. Roy has studied his recordings, heard him in person, and hopes to have a lesson from him one day.

In a sense the Deffinbaughs also see music as a gift you can give to yourself because it is so therapeutic. Phyllis recalls times when she "just needed to sit down and play and pound and maybe cry a little." Roy, a bit more analytical, says music is therapeutic because it demands all your cerebral efforts. He reasons that if you're concentrating

SAGE ADVICE

♦♦♦♦♦

Why not pray about your involvement in your community? Start talking to your friends at church. Look in the community papers. See if anyone is looking for help. The nursing homes love to have people come in and sing. The reception you get will make you think you're the best in the world.

ROY AND PHYLLIS DEFFINBAUGH

100 percent, it's impossible to worry at the same time. Time free from worrying leaves you refreshed.

While music has become their main hobby in their post-teaching years, the Deffinbaughs believe it's important to lead a balanced life. At home in Shelton, Washington, their day begins with a two-mile walk by the lake that fronts their home. Afterward it's weight lifting time for Roy in the exercise room he built at the water's edge. Furnished with a wood-burning stove and a comfortable reading chair, the room can be used for spiritual and mental exercise as well as for physical. Roy admits that some of his friends think he is a fanatic because he lifts weights five days a week. But he defends his practice as part of the balanced Christian life. "If you don't read, your mind goes south; if you don't exercise, the body falls apart. It makes it difficult to carry on." The Deffinbaughs work hard at maintaining necessary balance.

By Deffinbaugh definition, maintaining balance requires discipline. Just as every at-home day begins with an exercise routine, so it ends with an hour of practice on their instruments. Roy goes through a

warm-up ritual before Phyllis joins him. They play classical, pop, and sacred music. They also play contest pieces,
something serious soloists might play.

Rehearsing and performing with other groups keeps the
Deffinbaugh calendar crammed. Although Phyllis doesn't
always participate, she goes with Roy. He names all the
local groups in which he participates:

- The Rhythmaires—made up of harmonica, keyboard,
  bass guitar, and Roy's trombone. They entertain once a
  week on a rotating basis at a nursing home and a senior
  center. Through their church the Deffinbaughs play at
  another senior center once a month.
- The American Legion band in Olympia. They rehearse
  weekly and perform between ten and fifteen times a year.
  Since it's the only American Legion band in the north-
  west, they usually play at the annual state convention.
- A brass quintet and a trombone quartet within the
  American Legion band.
- A German band that plays authentic oompah music.
- A circus band that plays circus tunes.

In between all these obligations Roy volunteers his
time in public schools. Formerly a history and social studies teacher, he now works with budding musicians in
middle school bands.

Their yearly schedule includes trips to Elderhostel music
programs and masters programs for musicians. They attend
the latter as auditors, avoiding the qualifying process
required of those who participate in the actual teaching
program. The instructor gives a lesson to five different
musicians playing five different instruments. As auditors,
Roy and Phyllis sit in on private lessons and hear the
critiques made by the instructor.

Meeting friends outside their church is one of the pluses Phyllis sees in their music involvement. She enjoys meeting people they would never have met outside the music world. On the other hand, the Deffinbaughs believe it is important to keep up with friends they have known for many years.

Every year they make two major efforts to keep in touch with old friends: They host a reunion at the lake for all their friends from the youth group they attended as teenagers, and they take a three-week trip through California and Arizona, visiting family and friends from college days. If they happen to be staying with friends who have a piano, they get in their hour of practice there. If not, Roy goes looking for a church and asks, "Would you allow us to use your piano for an hour?" Keeping up with music doesn't allow for slacking, even when you're on vacation. Practice not only makes perfect, it ensures that the music never stops.

Contacts:

Elderhostel, Inc.
11 Avenue de Lafayette
Boston, MA 02111-1746
www.elderhostel.org

Elderhostel, Inc.
P. O. Box 4488 Station A
Toronto, Ontario M5W4H1

CHAPTER **6**

✦Researching Syntax instead of Symptoms

*F*IVE mornings a week, eighty-seven-year-old Dr. William Nesbitt goes to his office. He opens the miniblinds to allow light into the wood-paneled room, then takes his place behind a computer. A stack of over-flowing file boxes sits on a counter behind the doctor's chair. At his elbow is a row of reference volumes. Notice-ably missing are the examination table, the blood-pressure monitor, and the medicine samples.

These days when the doctor goes to his office (conve-niently located in his home), he isn't searching for exact cures. He's searching for exact words. When he pauses to consult a reference book, it's not to verify symptoms, it's to check his syntax. Two years ago William began a new career. He became a freelance writer.

After launching his career with a *Guideposts* magazine article about his wife, Bernice, who suffers from dementia, he has chalked up more than a dozen sales to major magazines. At an age when most people would spend their day reading a good book, William is attempting to write one.

Although William refers to writing as his "seventh career," it might be more accurate to say that he moon-lights as a writer while he makes a career of caring for his wife of more than fifty years.

SAGE ADVICE

✦✦✦✦✦

If you're going to meet whatever challenges may come, you must take care of your health. Eat a well-balanced diet. Get the proper amount of rest. Most of all, exercise your brain by doing creative activities.

DR. WILLIAM NESBITT

For eight years, since the onset of Bernice's illness, William has faced a daily challenge to find time for his needs as well as hers. With careful planning and practical arrangements, he has managed to strike a balance between the two. For five days a week, he employs a caregiver and makes use of a nearby adult day-care facility. Only on weekends is he solely responsible for his wife.

William plans his week around Bernice's schedule since she can never be left alone. On weekends he gives her his full attention, never letting her out of his sight, even in their yard with its high redwood fence. Weekdays, while Bernice is in the day-care facility, William does household errands as well as writing. He also exercises at a fitness club three to five afternoons a week.

The caregiver comes five mornings a week to get Bernice ready for the day. Afterward William delivers his wife to an adult day-care facility. He brings her home at five, prepares her evening meal, and puts her to bed.

With ready praise for the day-care facility, William recalls that this seemingly perfect arrangement was not available in the early years of his wife's illness. Rather than bemoan the town's lack, he pounded on a few doors, bent a few ears, and lobbied for a local adult day-care facility. When he brought the need to the attention of his church, the church agreed to provide space. A local nonprofit organization assumed responsibility for the rest.

Once a year Bernice goes to a residential care facility for a week while William attends a writers' conference. From breakfast to bedtime he attends workshops, talks with editors, and pitches his latest literary brainstorms. He attributes his ability to maintain a rigorous schedule to family genes and to the promise of God. "My grace is sufficient for thee . . . my strength is made perfect in weakness," he quotes, then adds that this verse (2 Corinthians 12:9, KJV) has sustained him throughout his wife's illness.

A few years short of ninety, William describes his life as one that has been filled with both change and challenge. His eyes flash with excitement as he talks about his latest challenge—to perfect the craft of writing. He has every intention of leaving his mark on the publishing world as well as on the medical world.

Contacts:
For seniors wishing to explore a writing career, check *Christian Writers' Market Guide* by Sally E. Stuart. Updated annually, published by Harold Shaw, the book includes a list of workshops and conferences for aspiring writers.

CHAPTER **7**

✦From Choral Director to Chorus Composer

*I*N spite of the hearing aids he is forced to wear these days, Carroll Carruth has the perpetual look of an adventure-seeking little boy. Hardly ever without a smile, his eyes twinkle as he talks about his passion—composing music. For the past four years Carroll has been involved in a composing project that is reaching around the world. Judging from his enthusiasm, one would expect to hear about something grandiose. Instead, with eyes still twinkling, he explains that he is writing a series of short songs for a missionary friend in Romania.

Carroll, who holds a doctorate in music, spent his working years teaching music at the college level and directing community choruses and church choirs, but he rarely had time for composing. There was one notable exception: He was commissioned by the Arizona Commission on the Arts and Humanities to write a historical musical to celebrate the five hundredth anniversary of the conquistadors coming to Yuma, Arizona. He recalls the challenging project with excitement but prefers to talk about his current project, which he finds no less exciting.

He met Rita, a missionary to Romania, in Pagosa Springs, Colorado, where the Carruths have a summer home. After Rita and her husband went to Romania as

SAGE ADVICE

✦✦✦✦✦

You husbands, do your share of the household chores so your wife can "retire" too. Keep active in church and in your field of expertise. Don't spend all your playtime with other seniors. Learn how to be a grandparent or a special friend to kids and young people. Be available to them for advice and just for fun.

DR. CARROLL CARRUTH

missionaries, she saw a need to teach English to the people. In conjunction with a publisher in the U.S., she began to develop a curriculum. In the process she called upon Carroll to come to her aid.

"I need a song for every letter of the alphabet," she said. She admitted she was concerned about the letter X, but Carroll, eager to take on the project, assured her they could do a song about Xerxes.

A computer expert as well as a musician, Carroll composes by means of a computer keyboard and keeps in touch with Romania by e-mail. Whether wintering in Arizona or spending summers in Colorado, he logs a good many hours at his computer. He has composed nearly fifty short songs. Sometimes he writes both the words and the music, sometimes he collaborates with Rita on the words, and sometimes he uses Scripture.

"I love to set the Scripture to music," he says. Currently he is working on Paul's doxology in the last four verses of Romans 11.

Carroll's interest in computers has enabled him to move forward on the composing project. (He holds lifetime teacher certification in Arizona for both music and computers.) At first he sent his songs to the publisher by "snail mail" every week at a cost of five to ten dollars. When he suggested that they could take care of it by e-mail, the publishing company's secretary was skeptical. With Carroll's urging, she agreed to try. Now he sends music, score, and words all by e-mail.

Like many active seniors, Carroll's willingness to accept change and try new things has prepared him for the challenges he now faces. While he was teaching at Arizona Western College in Yuma, Arizona, Carroll decided to get into electronic music. Computerized music was just being introduced. He took summer workshops at Dartmouth and Stanford. He established a computer music lab at AWC, one of the first such labs in the smaller colleges. Forever growing in his field, he is well prepared to combine computer technology with music skills for a second career in composing.

His post-teaching years have brought opportunities to teach computer and to lead both adult and children's choirs. Currently he is directing a children's choir in his Pagosa Springs community. Between music projects he finds time to take preteen boys to summer camp. But he continues to devote most of his time to composing, the one thing for which he never had time before.

CHAPTER **8**

✦Traveling against All Odds

*E*RIKA PRECHTL lives alone on a pleasant, tree-lined street in Novato, California The sidewalk borders a well-manicured lawn and leads directly to a shaded entryway where there are numerous potted plants but no steps. Double wooden doors provide an extra large entry, and at the ring of the bell, Erika appears, pushing her walker before her. In the garage, out of sight, is Erika's Ford Taurus, complete with a trailer on which sits her scooter.

Now in her mid-seventies, Erika is a polio survivor who contracted the disease when she was three months old. Although always crippled, she is quick to point out that she was never handicapped until some fifteen years ago. At that time she began walking with a cane. Then came the scooter. Then came the walker. She accepts each one as a welcome aid to mobility. Erika is a world traveler, and she intends to continue traveling as long as possible.

Driving is her passion. Whether visiting relatives in Germany or taking a friend to the San Francisco airport, she is undaunted by strange roads or congested freeways. She learned to drive as a young adult. After work one hot, humid day as she rode the bus home, she was challenged by an advertisement from the Webster School of Driving. The ad pictured a horse sitting behind the wheel of a car

SAGE ADVICE

✦✦✦✦✦

You can't dwell on what you have lost or what is past. You have to look forward, and when you look forward you can accomplish whatever you set your mind to do. That's what I've done all my life.

If you want to go someplace, check it out to see what's available. It's amazing how many helps are available to people who have handicaps. There are far more than you will ever dream.

ERIKA PRECHTL

and grinning from ear to ear. The caption read, "If you can get into a car, we can teach you to drive." Mentally, Erika dared the school to prove it. "I said, 'By gum, you just show me!'" Two and a half weeks later she had her temporary driving license.

She remembers it as a watershed moment. When she realized that she was going to be able to drive, she saw doors opening to a new world. "From the minute I got into the car, there was nothing I liked better than to drive a car."

While Erika doesn't remember her childhood as being so different because of her disease, she does remember two things that set her apart from her peers in Montebello, California. In the Prechtl home only German was spoken. And Erika had no cousins, aunts, or uncles with whom she could spend vacations or holidays. They all lived in Germany. In Hamburg alone there were fifty-seven Prechtl relatives. Erika's parents kept in touch with their German relatives and that, in part, accounts for her love of travel. She has made ten trips to Germany and is dreaming about another in the not-too-distant future.

She remembers the first trip, made over thirty years ago with her mother. They had decided to go for a year while Erika was between jobs. As they were making plans they learned of a Hillman Minx car being test-driven from Alaska to the tip of Mexico. It was in Hollywood for a few days, available for trial runs by potential buyers. Erika went to check it out. "I got in that little Hillman Minx and just sailed all over the Hollywood hills." Convinced it was the right car for her, she made arrangements to take delivery on one in Paris. She put eighteen thousand miles on it before it ever left Europe.

In those days her biggest challenge was remembering her German. Getting around was not a problem. Getting around has become a problem in recent years, but it is not one that Erika is willing to give in to. For extended trips she always travels with a companion because it's too hard to manage motels on her own. Twice a year she travels to Montebello by herself. "I get in the car and eight hours later I am at my brother's home," she explains. Last year, with a companion, she traveled to her sixtieth high school reunion held in Las Vegas, Nevada. She made stops at the Grand Canyon and other northern Arizona destinations.

She points out that there are many helps available for handicapped travelers, not the least of which is the automatic transmission. Unable to lift her legs once she sits down, Erika cannot make the necessary moves between clutch and gas pedal. But with an automatic transmission she can pivot her heel and move her foot between gas and brake. From that early adjustment, Erika has continued to find aids for those who travel against all odds. On a trip to Washington, D.C., she discovered taxis that carry wheel-chairs and a rental company that provides scooters. With a rented scooter and a wheelchair-toting taxicab, Erika and her companion toured the nation's capitol, going "wherever we wanted to go."

The effects of post-polio syndrome have left Erika unable to do many of the things she did in the past. A favored soloist in her church, she no longer sings because of the disease's effect on her lungs. She has given up sewing because she can't hold the needle between thumb and forefinger. But she emphasizes that with her scooter she can still get around wherever she needs to go. When pressed on the question of travel, she declares, "I'm going to travel as long as I can." In August she plans to drive to Oregon with her godchild. And of course, in the back of her mind, there's always that next trip to Germany.

SPOTLIGHT
Caleb Claims a Mountain

There is something inspiring about the picture of an eighty-five-year-old man standing in the midst of men four decades younger, pleading for the chance to show what he can do. This was Caleb on a historic morning at the town of Gilgal, when the men of Judah approached Joshua. The fringes of the Promised Land had been conquered, and it was time to divide the land. Joshua, now in his eighties, faced the men, all at least forty years younger than himself.

All but one. Caleb, Joshua's contemporary, stood out among the crowd, not because he was aging and feeble but because he spoke boldly and with enthusiasm, making his pitch. He wanted Hebron. Hebron, the place he had investigated forty-five years earlier. A valley that lay three thousand feet above sea level and was surrounded by hills planted with vineyards. Hebron, with the brook of Eschol running quite near where Caleb and his companions had collected grapes and pomegranates and figs to present to Moses. Hebron, the place Moses had promised to Caleb because Caleb wholly followed the Lord even in the face of rebellion by ten of his companions.

Because of their rebellion, Caleb's dreams were put on hold. For more than forty years, he carried his dream. No whining, no complaining. Just waiting. Today he reached for it.

"Here I am today, eighty-five years old! I am still as strong today as the day Moses sent me out; I'm just as vigorous to go out to battle now as I was then. Now give me this hill country that the Lord promised me that day. . . . the Lord helping me, I will drive [the Anakites] out" (Joshua 14:11-12).

Obviously when an octogenarian speaks so boldly, there must be more than "talk" involved. When Caleb volunteered (demanded would be a better word) to conquer the Anakites at Hebron, he was fully prepared to take on the rigorous campaign. His past had prepared him for the present. Forty years of walking in the desert kept him in shape physically. Forty years of walking with the Lord kept him fit spiritually. There was nothing to prevent him from continuing to "wholly follow the Lord."

After Caleb's speech, the divine record makes this note: "Then the land had rest from war" (Joshua 14:15). Like Moses and Joshua, Caleb had an important part in the process. Unlike Moses, Caleb never questioned whether he was the man for the job. "God promised it to me. God has kept me strong. With God's help, I'll get the job done. Let me at it!"

✦ ✦ ✦ ✦ ✦

PART TWO

FOREVER HELPING OTHERS

*Allow me to introduce to you several dozen dynamic
people devoted to helping others. From various socioeconomic
backgrounds, they are all in what society calls the post-
retirement years. But they are not retired. They are busy in
their churches, in their communities, and in other countries.
Some travel widely. Some stay close to home. They write
music. They write computer programs. They write letters.
They paint buildings. They build camp dormitories. They stuff
envelopes and pray. They visit hospitals.
They teach women in Ghana how to run a business.
One, my good friend Steve Lazarian, helps impoverished
people of Armenia to survive one day at a time. Steve is the
epitome of what I think God can do with a dedicated individual
in that so-called "post-retirement" period. I have known him
for years. He served on the board of World Vision for a decade
and a half. During that time, he traveled with me to Tanzania
to visit one of our projects and made several practical
suggestions to the people for improving their conditions. On
that trip, I challenged Steve to give some of his time and talent
to helping people in Third World countries. Today, at age
seventy-eight, Steve makes three trips a year to Armenia,
supervising relief efforts that are tied to gospel witness*

programs. Because of his connection with World Vision, he has received over a million dollars of relief goods from World Vision for distribution in Armenia. For this significant partnership, Steve has expressed deep appreciation. Here is his story, followed by dozens of others— all about highly motivated people who are committed to helping others.

CHAPTER **9**

✦The Armenian Connection

*P*ASADENA businessman Steve Lazarian stood
at the edge of an Armenian soccer field and watched in
wonder as most of the audience surged forward in
response to a simple evangelistic message. Then, without
warning, he found himself staring at an angry young man
who shoved a finger in Steve's face and said, "God will
hold you accountable. You come with words, but nothing
of substance."

The year was 1991. Steve Lazarian, an American-born
Armenian, was sixty-eight, and this was his first visit to
the homeland of his ancestors. He and several other
laymen had gone to Armenia seeking opportunities for
evangelism. They set up informal meetings in sports
arenas and soccer fields and watched in amazement as the
people came forward to make decisions for Christ or to
ask the Americans to pray for them. Then the young man
stuck his finger under Steve's nose, and Steve's life has
never been the same since.

Today, some ten years later, Steve and his wife, Iris, are
widely known as a couple who devote their time and
money to caring for the impoverished people of Armenia.
Under the auspices of the Armenian Gospel Mission
(AGM), Steve is heavily involved in projects that allow

SAGE ADVICE

✦✦✦✦✦

***A* lot of passion comes with going to observe a need. From there you find your gifts and skills to meet that need.**

STEVE LAZARIAN

him to speak to the Armenians about Christ while ministering to them "with substance."

With some thirty visits to Armenia behind him, Steve admits that the lesson learned in 1991 has shaped all his subsequent visits. On that first trip, the men were thrilled at the openness of the people, but they were woefully unprepared for any lasting ministry. They had no Bibles, no follow-up material of any kind, nothing to share but their spoken words. Steve had no rebuttal for the angry young man who disappeared into the crowd, never to be seen again. The incident turned an exhilarating experience into a humiliating lesson. He never again went to Armenia without thinking about the need for substance.

As he made numerous return trips to Armenia, he discovered people on the very edge of starvation. He visited whole villages where people lived in shanties, converted oil tankers, and freight containers. The latter, called *domiks*, were furnished by the government as temporary shelters when a quarter of a million people lost their homes in the 1988 earthquake. Gutted hulks of high-rise buildings made a stark background for row upon row of rusting freight containers where thirty-five thousand people made their homes.

On a winter day when temperatures dipped to near zero, Steve and his wife, Iris, visited a family of ten living in an unheated domik with icicles hanging from the ceiling. In another domik they found an old woman who could not get out of bed because she had not eaten in days.

In 2000, in an effort to bring substance along with words to Armenia, the AGM took volunteers from the United States on a work/witness program. They visited two thousand of the poorest people, including many who lived in domiks. The teams distributed "Power Paks"— specially designed canvas bags that contained an Armenian Bible, a "Bridge of Life" tract, clothing or shoes, aspirin, soap, towels, toiletries, and money valued at about twenty U.S. dollars.

A short time after the Power Paks were distributed, trained follow-up teams of young Armenian men and women visited the recipients. They initiated Bible studies, prayed with the people, and sought to meet spiritual needs.

Combining substance with words led to a ministry with children that continues to be the largest and most effective area of emphasis by the AGM. Children of Armenia benefit from distribution programs in which they receive school supplies, textbooks, medicine, and shoes. More than sixty thousand pairs of shoes have been donated to date. When mothers cannot feed, clothe, or give adequate care to their hungry children and there is no father in the home, the children become social orphans. The AGM has five schools that care for both the spiritual and physical needs of social orphans. Nearly six hundred such children are cared for ten hours every day on a year-round basis.

Steve concedes that he is, at one level or another, involved in a dizzying number of projects. From 100,000 Armenian Bibles to ten freight containers of hospital supplies to 15,000 undergarments for women and children, there is always something that needs to be sent from the U.S. to Armenia.

The relief programs in Armenia are facilitated through

an AGM subsidiary humanitarian foundation in Armenia, of which Steve serves as U.S. board president. He emphasizes that the projects are about more than relief. Every project must have a dimension of strategic evangelism to it, lest substance is emphasized to the exclusion of words.

At home in Pasadena, California, he still works ten to twelve hours per day. He continues to make at least three trips each year to Armenia. But he knows the limits of an aging leader for a growing organization with a staggering number of projects. He expects to have a successor in the next two years but will continue to work for the spiritual and physical needs of Armenia so long as God gives him strength.

He says, "It has been our prayer and desire that through the years God would be honored by the use of our professional skills as well as tangible assets." That would explain why a man who is almost eighty spends so much time and money helping others. But in part, Steve's motivation can be attributed to the memory of an angry young man who stuck a finger under Steve's nose and said, "God will hold you accountable."

CHAPTER **10**

✦Looking Both Ways from a Suspension Bridge

ALL my life I would say, 'Here I am Lord, use me,' and He would say, 'Not yet.' And when I said, 'Life is over, I'm old and worn out,' then He said, 'Now I can use you.'"

The words tumbled out as eighty-year-old Barbara Hudson paused for a few minutes in her packing. Standing in the living room of her Thousand Oaks, California, home, she explained that an unexpected opportunity had prompted a move that would take her from one coast to the other. Outwardly calm in spite of the two-day departure deadline, she admitted, "I feel like I'm standing in the middle of a suspension bridge and looking both ways."

Looking forward, Barbara saw an incredible opportunity to use her drama talents on Hilton Head Island, South Carolina, if she was willing to pull up stakes and move across the country. Looking backward, she saw all her past experience as a time of preparation for this new opportunity.

Barbara Hudson has been involved in drama all her life. She holds a master's degree in the field from USC. She helped with the production of Billy Graham films. She produced pageants at the Hollywood Presbyterian Church for sixteen years. She taught drama for eighteen

SAGE ADVICE

✦✦✦✦✦

Churches, remember that seniors have the wealth, the time, and the experience. They should be serving more than anybody. Keep them involved in the loop of the church. Seniors, don't look back. Don't yearn over what was. With God's strength, accept the present conditions, difficult though they may be.

BARBARA HUDSON

years at a church college and toured with a drama group for a dozen years or so, writing all their material. She has had eighteen church dramas published. Throughout her long career, she saw drama as a tool for evangelism. "It's never been just for entertainment," she emphasizes.

She was past sixty-five when the idea came to her to develop a series of monologues on women of the Bible. Her career years were behind her—years of writing, directing, producing. She often found herself thinking that her life was over. One evening as she sat outside poking through the dying embers in her fire pit, she glanced at the open Bible lying on her lap. There she read the verse, ". . . fan into flame the gift of God which is in you" (2 Timothy 1:6). *That's interesting,* she thought. *I'm sitting here stirring the ashes and I should be fanning into flames my gift. What is my gift?*

The answer was simple. Barbara always knew that her gift was acting. But at her advanced years, what could she do with it? Shortly after the incident at the fire pit, she conceived the idea to write her monologues on women of the Bible.

She admits to a false start when the question of age entered the picture. Thinking that she would start with Eve, she sat down at her typewriter and typed, "I am Eve." But she couldn't go any further. "No one ever talks about Eve after she ate the apple," Barbara says, "and I thought, how can I be Eve? I'm old. I've waited too long."

After further consideration, she decided to write Eve as an aged woman looking back on her life and all that she lost in Eden. Barbara's message to the audience was "Don't look back. Live in the present."

She wrote forty-nine more monologues in which she portrayed women of the Bible grown old, looking back upon their lives. In churches and conference centers, biblical women came alive when the tall, statuesque, elderly woman appeared on stage in full costume and flawlessly presented her program.

Through a chain of events that began with an appearance at a West Coast writers' conference and ended with an appearance on the East Coast, Barbara was invited to come to Hilton Head Island to assist with a church drama program. Specifically, she was asked to prepare presentations for the two and a half million visitors who come to the island during the summer. When she met with the church staff to discuss the possibility, she asked, "Do you realize I'm eighty years old?"

"So was Moses when he led the children of Israel through the desert to the Promised Land," the rector replied.

They agreed to a three-month trial.

Early one May morning, Barbara loaded everything into her car and began a five-day trek across country, driving solo. On the day before departure, she e-mailed a few friends the following message:

"I'm following the yellow brick road in the morning, going east to Hilton Head, Lord willing. I figure that He parted the Red Sea, brought down the walls of Jericho, and quite a few other miracles, so He should be able to get my car loaded and on the way. It's difficult with all the questions swimming in my mind. . . ."

At departure time she still didn't have the answer to the most nagging question of all: "Why me, Lord? Why am I doing this?" With questions and baggage alike she headed out. Several days later, somewhere around Hammond, Indiana, the answer became clear. In a sudden moment of insight, Barbara understood. "I'm eighty years old and I am the perfect one to present the claims of Christ to all the other seniors who have gone all the way through their lives and careers ignoring Him." Just as she had done all her life, so she would do on Hilton Head Island. She would use drama as a tool for evangelism.

At times on the rest of her journey she still felt as though she was standing in the middle of a suspension bridge, but she looked only one way—straight ahead. There an exciting opportunity awaited the woman who had once told God, "I'm old and worn out," and heard Him say, "Now I can use you."

CHAPTER **11**

✦Discovering Gold
among the Aspens

WITH their teaching careers behind them,
college professors Cory and Monroe Hughbanks packed
their bags in preparation for a fall vacation. Colorado
during the time of yellowing aspen awaited them. It had
been forty-six years since they honeymooned there, and
they had dreamed about it every year as they dug into the
fall quarter at McPherson College in McPherson, Kansas.

Now, on a hot, dry mid-September morning, they loaded
their four-year-old Oldsmobile, locked the door of their
ranch-style house, and headed west via the back roads of
western Kansas and eastern Colorado. Four hundred and
forty miles later, they arrived in Colorado Springs, checked
into a motel, and fell into bed. Little did they dream that as
they went in search of aspen they would discover another
career.

The next day, on the spur of the moment, they decided
to stop by Focus on the Family headquarters to see Gary
Lydic, a former McPherson College student. As they
toured the facilities with Gary, he asked them, "Why
don't you do some volunteer work here?" By January the
Hughbanks were back at Focus on the Family headquarters, working for the month. They have returned two or
three times a year ever since.

SAGE ADVICE

✦✦✦✦✦

Don't sit and wait for somebody to come and offer you a position. Go for it. Make contact with the group you are interested in and pursue it. It takes initiative, but once you push the first domino down, the opportunities come like a flood.

CORY AND MONROE
HUGHBANKS

Now starting their seventh year, the Hughbanks fill a variety of needs. Monroe frequently is found entering data into the computer. He recalls one project in which he spent two weeks gleaning statistics from a survey and feeding them into the computer. Cory's most frequent responsibility is telephone reception work. But Cory also spends days stapling papers and putting packets together for conferences—"piddly" but necessary work.

While their volunteer work is vastly different from the lesson planning and lecturing they once did, the Hughbanks enjoy the diversity it presents. Whether performing humble behind-the-scenes jobs or visible up-front jobs, they float all over the ministry. According to Monroe, regular employees sometimes comment to the Hughbanks, "You know more about the ministry than we do." He acknowledges there is truth in the statement because where employees are necessarily focused on one small area of concern, he and Cory are exposed to many areas, which gives them a wider view of the ministry.

The Hughbanks plan their thrice-annual visits to Focus on the Family around the organization's conference schedule, making every effort to be in Colorado Springs for large conferences of eight hundred or more. Chances are, the Hughbanks will be the first faces incoming conferees see. Monroe and Cory are on hand at the airport to welcome arrivals. They serve as a two-person orientation committee, giving directions, handing out maps, providing lists of what to do, and answering dozens of questions.

The Hughbanks echo the advice of many of their peers regarding health challenges. A physical problem doesn't mean it's time to quit; rather, it's time to readjust. In the beginning, Monroe and Cory came for a month at a time and worked forty hours per week. But after Monroe suffered a heart attack, they decided to cut down. Now they come for about three weeks and work thirty hours per week.

At home in McPherson, Kansas, the Hughbanks keep busy with other volunteer projects. Both volunteer at their local hospital. Cory works at the gift shop or the information desk. Monroe does backup work for the chaplain.

Unable to resist the call of the open road, Monroe and Cory also act as tour directors with a Christian tour agency. On the bus tours, Monroe leads the devotions every morning, setting the tone for the trip. Although the tour company arranges for guides at scheduled stops, the Hughbanks do research on the route and provide basic information on the destinations.

If their teaching careers prevented fall vacations in search of golden aspen, those same careers allowed the Hughbanks to do summer volunteer work. By the time Gary Lydic suggested to the Hughbanks that they do volunteer work at Focus on the Family, they had given many summers to Team Missions International of Merritt Island, Florida. They spent a summer in Bolivia, one in Finland, one in Poland, and two in the kitchen at the Florida headquarters. In spite of their accumulated experience, they responded to Lydic's suggestion with, "But we don't know anything about it."

Wannabe volunteers who feel hesitant to step up to the plate should take courage from the fact that sometimes even seasoned volunteers are initially reluctant. But the Hughbanks point out that after they took the plunge they discovered once again that much of volunteer work is learned on the job. After seven years they still agree that their search for gold among the aspen ended with a golden opportunity to serve the Lord.

CHAPTER **12**

✦ The Doctor Is In

*A*N ARTICLE in his hometown newspaper identified Kirk Stetson as the "retired physician who has dedicated much of his life to serving others." The "serving others" part is accurate, but one can hardly refer to Kirk as "retired." Kirk himself is quick to tell you that he loves "retirement," but it's obvious that he has his own definition of the word. "I can go to bed at night and not have to worry about the telephone waking me for some emergency." Sleeping through the night seems to be the only difference retirement has brought to this tall, quiet, unassuming man.

In his "post-retirement" years, Kirk spent eighteen months working in five separate African countries and five years working for a clinic in the bottom of Havasu Canyon, which is often described as the Indian Shangri-la of the Grand Canyon. He remembers his time in the canyon as hard work with a lot of responsibility. Getting there was always an ordeal. He went in for periods of one to three weeks at a time. When the helicopter landed with Kirk, his wife, Bunnie, and their two hundred pounds of luggage and food, the Supai Indians knew that the doctor was in.

Currently Kirk works "on call" with a clinic on the

✦✦✦✦✦

If you are looking for volunteer work, you should begin with your own church. Inquire what mission boards are offering in America or overseas.

DR. KIRK STETSON

Hualapai reservation, which he finds less grueling than the Havasu Canyon clinic. Instead of descending into the village by helicopter, he drives over the brow of a hill down several steep grades into the town of Peach Springs (population 1,000). Always arriving by night, he is greeted by twinkling lights of the village where the "people of the tall pines" live.

The first houses to come into view are four double-wide trailers all painted white and placed in a row. These buildings are the administration office and the living quarters for clinic personnel. Kirk pulls up beside the fourth trailer, which is reserved for the visiting doctor. At the other end of the block stands the clinic itself. Rectangular in appearance and fronted by a single facade, it is actually a series of double-wide trailers converted into a clinic. Nearby are an ambulance and a helicopter pad to accommodate the emergency medical service that takes over at 5:00 P.M. every day. At that time residents of Peach Springs know that the visiting doctor is no longer in.

At home in Cottonwood, Arizona, seventy-five-year-old Kirk maintains a full regimen of study, hobbies, and volunteer duties. He gives one morning a week to a local clinic for the working uninsured and serves as medical advisor for a mission that is working to establish a free clinic. He serves as chairman of the local chapter of Habitat for Humanity, teaches a weekly men's Bible study,

serves on his church missions committee, and still finds
time for educational pursuits. He attends noon seminars
at the local hospital and devotes one afternoon a week to
the review of medicine and Spanish.

Kirk explains his involvement with Habitat for Humanity as an opportunity to put faith into action. "My guiding
light is my Christian faith," he says. A background in engineering is also partly responsible for his long involvement
with Habitat for Humanity. An early interest in missions
prompted him to study engineering. He reasoned that engineering plus a knowledge of agriculture would help him
demonstrate faith in action to Third World people. Today
he admits that while he used engineering during his seventeen years as a missionary, it was "more ingenuity than
engineering."

Kirk and Bunnie spent seventeen years as medical
missionaries in Zimbabwe, Africa. "We've been gone
thirty years," he says, "and there hasn't been a week that
we haven't had a letter from over there, which means
that I have a heavy load of letter writing. I am very keen
to keep in touch with people."

"Keeping in touch" encompasses more than letter writing. Currently the Stetsons are helping support a young
African student. This involvement explains, in part, why
Kirk sought "post-retirement employment." His salary
from the Peach Springs clinic goes toward the support of
the African student.

Kirk does not hesitate to ask others, even seniors like
himself, to become involved as volunteers. A survivor of
bypass surgery, he stresses that health problems that come
with aging should not prevent one from volunteering.
"Just because you have health setbacks doesn't mean
you're put on the bench."

Kirk Stetson may be known about Cottonwood as "a

retired physician," or, in some circles, as "a retired missionary." But those who know him best protest that he has retired from neither.

Contacts:

The Christian Medical and Dental Associations
P. O. Box 7500
Bristol, TN 37621-9920
www.cmdahome.org

World Medical Mission
A ministry of Samaritan's Purse
P. O. Box 3000
Boone, NC 28607
(828) 262-1980
Fax: (828) 266-1053
www.samaritanspurse.org

CHAPTER **13**

✦Called to Mentor

*R*UBY FRERICHS'S townhouse is filled with mementos from her travels in Europe and limited-access countries: a treasured tea set, Russian nesting dolls, figurines and hats from many places. Her table linens are from Hungary, the china cups and plates from various cities. But it is the view from the window of her Denver duplex that evokes the most vivid memories of her years in faraway places. Sitting at her dining-room table she looks out upon the manicured lawns and remembers places where lawns are almost nonexistent. Gazing at the variety of houses in her neighborhood she remembers towns where thousands of look-alike gray apartments lined the streets. As she grabs her keys and heads for the car she remembers the long waits at cold bus stops and the crowded rides that followed. Or the numerous trips she made on planes that were in questionable condition.

A few years ago Ruby was traveling forty-five thousand miles a year into Eastern Europe and limited-access countries, where she assisted with the education needs of the children of expatriates who lived there. Today that part of the world is behind her. She only has to travel halfway across the city to meet with a young mentoree from Denver Seminary. She checks her Day Runner for the

My great joy would be to see many others of the finishers' generation out there using their skills for Him who gave them the skills in the first place.

RUBY FRERICHS

day's agenda, which may or may not be followed. A mentoring session, like life itself, has a way of taking its own direction.

Ruby has faced her senior years with a double-sided call upon her life—missions and mentoring. She admits that although her commitment to missions goes back to college, she always felt her mission field was the public-school setting where she taught for thirty-nine years. Now she sees those years as preparation for her recent stint as an educator overseas.

As for mentoring, Ruby has done this on an informal basis for years. She believes her singleness has opened doors for her to cultivate friendships with young, single females. Many have been encouraged by observing Ruby's success as a woman without a husband. In Denver she frequently has dinner individually with two "twentysomething" young women. Through visiting, shopping, and browsing in bookstores, she acts as an informal mentor to them.

Through Denver Seminary she mentors on a more formal basis. The seminary requires all students to be in a mentoring situation for at least three semesters, for which they receive one credit per semester. A highly structured program, it has definite requirements.

Ruby still lived overseas at the time her friend Dr. Terry Burns approached her to become a mentor through the seminary. While visiting in the area, Burns learned that Ruby was finalizing plans to move back to the States.

He asked her on the spot to join the mentoring program. Back in Denver a few months later, Ruby attended a four-hour mentor orientation and soon afterward was assigned to a young woman student.

Because the seminary requires the mentoree to write out goals for each semester, the area of focus is predetermined. With her mentoree, Ruby discusses strategies for change, looks at challenges, gives feedback and encouragement, guides in self-assessment, and periodically shares her own experiences.

For an hour each week Ruby meets with her mentoree. Because they live on opposite sides of the city they have tried various meeting places. Not all places have been conducive to a prayer time, so they continue to explore suitable options.

Ruby had assumed that her background would mean students in the missions or education field would be assigned to her. Instead, she was assigned one who was from the counseling program. "We bonded quickly," Ruby said, recognizing it as God's plan all along.

Recognizing God's plan as opposed to her own has been a part of Ruby's life. As a student she told the Lord that she was willing to go overseas if that was what He wanted. But she never felt the call to go until much later in life. Throughout her teaching years she developed friendships with many people who were serving the Lord overseas. One couple from Faith Academy in the Philippines frequently asked her to take a sabbatical and teach at Faith for one year. Her inability to tolerate hot, humid weather seemed to rule out this option. Later, when asked to go to Japan, she reluctantly told God she would go if He wanted her there. Privately she resisted this choice because on a previous visit she had found that being tall and blond made her stand out to the point of being uncomfortable.

When the opportunity came for an overseas ministry it was for a two-year commitment at the Vienna Christian School in Austria. Ruby stretched it into three years, working first as a middle school teacher and then as principal.

Back in Denver, she wondered if God had another overseas assignment for her. Soon she was asked to go as an educator to Eastern Europe and limited-access countries for one year. Again, the initial commitment turned into three years. She traveled to places that ten years earlier she didn't know existed, couldn't pronounce, and couldn't spell. She still travels to Hungary twice a year to serve on the board of directors for the organization with which she worked while living there.

Asked whether she would go again, Ruby answers enthusiastically, "Yes! Never in my wildest dreams would I imagine the joy that the Lord gave me as I served these people through educational issues for their children."

For now Ruby is content that mentoring is God's call upon her life. But just as she is never sure what direction a mentoring session will take, so she is never quite certain what direction her life will take at some future date.

CHAPTER **14**

✦Parenting the Second Time Around

*E*ULA JENKINS relaxes beneath one of her oil paintings (a California landscape) as she explains how she and her husband, Ervin, found a practical way to help their daughter, who is a single mom with two children.

"We were all living here," Eula said with a sweep of her hand, "and someone was sleeping in every room. Erv had his office in the garage and I had no place for my painting and my sewing."

Initially, the best solution seemed to be to buy a bigger house. But when the perfect one came along, Eula had second thoughts. She walked through the two family rooms, three bathrooms, and five bedrooms and wondered who would be cleaning all those bathrooms and climbing all those stairs.

"I knew it would be me," she recalls, "and I can't do that." They revised their plans, found a small house nearby, and purchased it for their daughter. Now everyone has their own space and Eula and Ervin are easily accessible for child-care responsibilities.

Caring for grandchildren on a year-round basis has been the primary challenge for Erv and Eula in their senior years. Eula describes their child-caring responsibilities as the most important work they do. Erv believes it is

SAGE ADVICE

✦✦✦✦✦

*I*nasmuch as possible, continue doing the things you love to do. If you believe God has thrust a responsibility upon you, commit yourself to the task and seek to keep balance in your life.

EULA JENKINS

what God would have them do at this stage of their lives, so he tries to do it as the Scripture teaches— enthusiastically with all his might. At the same time, he freely admits that it is hard work that continues to get harder.

When asked whether they had energy problems keeping up with a nine-year-old boy and an eleven-year-old girl, the Jenkinses both laughed. "Haven't you heard? They're having an energy crisis [in northern California] and we're it!"

Both in their seventies, the Jenkinses admit that parenting the second time around is not the same as the first time around. They can't always do the same things with their grandchildren as they did with their children. But they keep trying.

Recently Eula discovered to her surprise that she could no longer jump rope. She was turning the rope for the children when, on an impulse, she decided to trade places with one of them. "I can do that," she announced. "I was a good rope jumper." She managed to get in but then found that she couldn't jump.

Eula and Erv laugh at the limitations of age and say they have no intention of giving up their child-care responsibilities. They see it is as something that has to be done and something that would not be done by anyone else.

With careful planning over the past ten years, the Jenkinses have established a routine that works well for everyone. Their daughter drops the children off every morning on her way to work. Eula feeds them breakfast. They read from a children's Bible, and then Erv takes them to school. After school he picks them up, joins them in a little outside recreation, and then helps the grandson with his homework. When their single-mom daughter arrives after work, Eula has dinner on the table for everyone. After dinner, their daughter takes the children home and Eula and Erv have the evening for themselves.

Throughout the year the Jenkinses take the children on short excursions. At Thanksgiving time, they take the family to Disneyland or Knotts Berry Farm in southern California. During school vacations, Eula and Erv have the children all day. They plan outings with them, some-times taking a ride on the Skunk Train, sometimes camp-ing out for a few days in a nearby park.

Although this self-imposed responsibility toward the grandchildren is the main focus of their lives, Eula and Erv recognize the need for balance. They plan time for themselves as carefully as they plan outings for the chil-dren. Once each month they join long-time friends for a monthly potluck and game night. On those nights the children and their mother go out for hamburgers or take a pizza home. During the day while the children are in school Eula and Erv often go out for lunch. They make such times an ongoing priority. Getting a lunch date on the calendar gives them something to look forward to.

People who know Ervin and Eula Jenkins best often describe them as the couple who have laughed their way through life. Each has a great sense of humor, which served them well through a thirty-two-year pastorate in Santa Rosa, California. It continues to serve them as they, like a host of other grandparents, find themselves regularly caring for grandchildren. The difference between the Jenkinses and many others is that their practical approach to the situation has enabled them to maintain balance in their lives. By planning for themselves as well as for the children, Eula and Erv have found a way to make it work for everyone.

CHAPTER **15**

✦A Season for
Serving

*I*N November of 2000 a dream came true for
Dr. Al Diddams. He took a missions trip to Haiti.

During all his years of practice Al wanted to make such
a trip but found it difficult, if not impossible, to get away.
Now a youthful-looking seventy, he no longer works full-
time. When his son called and asked, "Would you like to
go to Haiti with me?" Al jumped at the chance.

The trip was sponsored by a Yakima, Washington–
based church. A small church with only about one
hundred people, they have sent sixty such teams over the
past twenty years to Haiti and to South America. "It is
just amazing what a few people who have a vision and
who are dedicated to it can achieve," Al observes.

The trips have always been medically related, and very
often the teams have returned year after year to the same
community. This was their tenth visit to the Haitian
community where Al helped set up a clinic. In the past,
the medical teams set up clinics wherever they could, but
Al's group used a church facility. The entire church came
to help, working as interpreters for the Creole-speaking
patients.

During his ten-day stay, Al and his five colleagues (two
doctors and three nurse practitioners) saw about 2,200

SAGE ADVICE

◆◆◆◆◆

If **you want to do something that has a lasting value for the Lord, you need to link up with a local church wherever you're going.**

DR. AL DIDDAMS

patients. He explains that the staggering caseload was possible because most of the patients suffered from the same maladies. They had malaria. They had parasites. They had various muscular skeletal problems from working in a perpetually bent-over posture.

The trip to Haiti confirmed one of Al's deepest convictions about short-term missions. He has long been convinced that the best way to ensure long-term benefits from short-term missions is to work through a national church. He points out that the church in Haiti is already established as a caring body in the area. He cites as an example the well on the church property that provides the only clean water in the neighborhood. In his opinion, the connection with the local church guarantees that the effects of any given project will continue long after the short-term missionaries have left the scene.

At the Haitian clinic the patients received not only free medicines but also rice and beans. Every year, in order to help the country's economy, the visiting team buys the rice and beans (five tons of each this year) in Haiti.

"Even sacking it up was a labor of love," Al recalls. "Someone had to work pretty hard."

We caught up with Al one rainy spring day and asked him what he did when he wasn't traveling to Haiti. He still works half days in endoscopy, ". . . looking into stomachs and colons and things like that." He shrugs and adds,

"No big deal." (Obviously spoken from the doctor's perspective rather than the patient's.)

For exercise he walks a mile and a half to an exercise room, lifts weights, then walks home again. He is a deacon in his church, he chairs one of the larger committees, and he and his wife, Sheila, host a growth group in their home. He describes the group as "half unbelievers and half from the church." Al teaches the group using Focus on the Family's "Faith Lessons on the Promised Land."

Always serving, Al is also always growing. He has some further education aspirations. To pursue one of his passions, he is considering embarking upon a formal education in bioethics with Trinity University in Deerfield, Illinois. "I don't plan to become some world-famous bioethicist," he explains, "but I want to be able to share the information with my friends and people in the church."

With five grown children scattered over the country, the Diddams find themselves on the road quite a bit. At this writing Al has not committed himself to return to Haiti next year, but he admits that this is a strong possibility.

CHAPTER **16**

✦On the Road
Again

*F*ORMER Los Angeles policeman Paul Duncan
and his wife, Millie, maintain a 2,800-square-foot home
in Arcadia, California, but for most of the year they live
in a thirty-four-foot fifth wheeler. Like many senior fifth-
wheel owners, the Duncans spend much of the year on
the road. Unlike recreation-seeking travelers, Paul and
Millie travel with a purpose.

When Paul retired from the police department, he and
Millie began a second career with Mobile Missionary
Assistance Program. For the past ten years they have
crisscrossed the country doing construction projects with
the organization. To date, the Duncans have completed
over sixty such projects.

On site, Millie is apt to be found doing office work, a
job for which she is uniquely suited through past experience with a department-store chain. Paul, on the other
hand, has learned a new trade altogether. Under the tute-
lage of senior builders in MMAP, Paul has become proficient at rough carpentry, framing, and sheet rock. In fact,
if needed, he lends a hand in almost any type of construction work except electrical.

The stated purpose of MMAP is to help churches, Bible
camps, Christian schools, and other Christ-centered

SAGE ADVICE

✦✦✦✦

When you
retire, you
have to have
something to
do. Fishing and
driving don't fill
the need. You
also have to
have something
to help continue
your witness.

PAUL AND MILLIE
DUNCAN

organizations with construction, remodeling, and repair. With a focus on building one might assume MMAP would prefer aging construction workers over other volunteers. Instead, the organization makes it clear that experience is not a requirement. The workers learn from each other. Howard Milligan, president of MMAP, says, "We believe if you make yourself available, the Lord will make you capable."

As members of MMAP, the Duncans are required to adhere to the basic principles, aim, and purpose of the organization. They are also required to do at least four projects a year. Paul and Millie currently do seven and are being trained to work at the MMAP headquarters.

Paul likes the exposure to the small communities where people are friendly and even the children come by to check the progress of MMAP workers. He particularly remembers the little town of Coarse Gold where one small boy spent a lot of time on the site visiting with the workers. Later when the boy bragged to his schoolteacher about the new church going up, his teacher asked, "Who is building it?" "I don't know," came the reply, "but there are a lot of grandmas and grandpas."

Paul emphasizes that the projects open up opportunities for workers to share their faith. Because everyone tends to know everyone else in a small town, the MMAP workers stand out wherever they go, affording them opportunities to answer questions and give witness.

Paul's personal exercise habit frequently opens doors for him. As a policeman he engaged in rigorous physical exercise, and he still works out as often as possible. "You'd be surprised how many of those small places have gyms," he says. His gray hair coupled with his ability to lift weights prompts questions from the locals.

While one of the pluses of working with MMAP is the opportunity to see more of the country, the Duncans tend to stay in the west with their projects. "We've been around the United States at least four times on our own," Paul explains. For the seven or eight months they are working with MMAP they are usually some place in Arizona, Nevada, or their home state of California.

Membership in MMAP is restricted to married couples who must have a self-contained recreational vehicle, be it motor home, trailer, or camper. They must be self-supporting and self-insured. Within ninety days after joining, members are required to work a project. At the time of joining and once a year thereafter, each member completes a form declaring in which months and in which region they plan to work during the coming year.

To assist them in making choices, members are provided with a map showing the regions in which MMAP works. Three regions are in the northern half of the United States (plus Canada and including Alaska), where the organization arranges projects from April through October. Three other regions are in the southern states and Mexico, where projects are done October through April. Projects are scheduled in three-week increments with members arriving on the first Friday of the month. They work an eight-hour day four days per week.

Many MMAP workers sell their homes and invest the

money in a motor home. Paul and Millie are able to retain their home because a daughter lives two doors away and can keep an eye on things for them. When not traveling they welcome the opportunity to spread out in their three-bedroom Arcadia home. They try to make the most of the interludes, knowing that soon they will be on the road again.

During one short period at home, a friend remarked to Millie, "You are earning stars in your crown with that wonderful work you do." Millie answered, "I don't think so. We are having too much fun!"

Paul agrees. "We are in our eleventh year with MMAP. I have no idea how long we will continue. We love it."

They may not always love living in a fifth wheeler, but they love traveling with a purpose.

Contacts:

Mobile Missionary Assistance Program
P. O. Box 725
Calimesa, CA 92320
(909) 795-3944

CHAPTER **17**

✦ Eighty-Year-Old Glue

*T*HE FIRST IMAGE one has of Margaret Pauley is that she is like the bunny with the drum that just keeps going and going and going. Becoming an octogenarian has not slowed her down. A petite woman who overflows with enthusiasm, she seems to have unlimited energy. For half a century she has been active in the First Baptist Church of Prescott, Arizona, and she sees no reason to change. To many who work with her, Margaret is like glue that holds things together.

She is the director for the annual Vacation Bible School, which draws three hundred students. While this may sound like a big task, Margaret describes it as an easy job because everyone wants to help. Each year as the Bible school closes the workers tell her, "Put me down for next year."

In addition to directing the summer Bible school, she teaches Sunday school in the junior department and serves as a volunteer on the church staff. She is also on the board of directors for Southwestern College in Phoenix. When asked what motivates her she says, "Well, you have to love what you do and you have to love people."

Margaret is enthusiastic about her job as staff volunteer. She meets with the pastoral staff every week to plan all the activities for the church of seven hundred-plus people.

SAGE ADVICE

✦✦✦✦✦

Don't wait to be asked. If there's something you would like to do, just go up and tell someone you would like to do it.

MARGARET PAULEY

"I get a dollar a year if they remember to pay me." She laughs over this and explains that it is strictly a volunteer position. It is, however, a position that requires many hours of service.

As staff volunteer Margaret is the social secretary of the church. She does all the weddings, all the dinners—anything that has to do with cooking. A sampling of those events includes MOPS program brunches, new members' receptions, Christmas class dinners, bereavement dinners, and the annual Thanksgiving dinner for all seniors. If the kitchen is open, Margaret is there.

A typical week begins at 6 A.M. on Sunday morning with Margaret in the church kitchen making coffee for the Sunday school classes. On Mondays she helps the young people in their soup-kitchen ministry. "I don't literally do the cooking," she explains. "I get things out and help the kids. It's their project but someone has to kind of give a little supervision." Tuesdays she attends a staff meeting. Wednesdays she describes as "my one time a week to go sit down. I go to a prayer meeting." On Thursdays she makes coffee for Bible study for the women's ministries.

Weekends bring the special events. Her eyes actually twinkle as she explains, "Friday and Saturday I do anything that comes along." It might be a men's breakfast or a supper for a visiting choir. During the annual missions festival it could be a luncheon for one hundred or a jungle party for two hundred.

When asked if being the social chairman for a church of that size amounted to a lot of work, Margaret smiles and replies with a great deal of enthusiasm, "I love it."

A widow, Margaret lives in the house she and her husband built nearly fifty years ago. One daughter lives with her and does day care in the home. Margaret explains her current situation as, "I'm free to come and go. I don't have a schedule I have to meet. If I need to be at the church, I'm there."

Her love for people prompts her to take on duties other than her official ones. Although not an official greeter, she stands at the front of the church and talks to people as they arrive. If she meets a new person looking for the right Sunday school class, she tries to connect them with the appropriate teacher. "I think you always have to be aware of the people around you. Many people just come to church and don't speak to others, but me—I've always been a glad-hander."

Obviously enjoying her senior years, Margaret explains the passion and purpose that exemplify her life. "You have to love the Lord first and then you love people. And I do love people."

Love the Lord, love people, and love what you are doing. That's the formula that keeps this octogenarian going and going and going.

SPOTLIGHT
A Circle of Silver-Haired Ladies

Becky Bell does not qualify as a subject for a book about seniors, but she has a dozen senior friends who are teaching her about sacrificial service. Becky is the Sunday school teacher for these women, who range in age from seventy-seven to ninety-one, but she protests that she learns more than she teaches in this class.

Every Sunday morning the women gather in a small room tucked in the corner of the Chilhowee Hills Baptist Church in Knoxville, Tennessee. They make no complaints about the metal folding chairs on which they must sit. The room is modestly appointed with a bulletin board, a small school desk for the class secretary, and a homemade podium. Week after week the room is filled with silver-haired ladies who have buried husbands, siblings, and children. Some can no longer drive or live alone, but all are active in service to God.

Becky describes the women as faithful. Faithful in attendance, faithful in tithing, faithful in prayer, faithful in reaching out to the unchurched of the community, and faithful in ministering to each other and to other church members. They are the first to provide food, flowers, and comfort to those who are ill or bereaved. They sing in the choir, serve on committees, participate in a twenty-four-hour prayer ministry and contribute financially to the ministry of the church.

One at a time or all together, the circle of silver-haired women demonstrates their determination to keep on serving until they draw their last breath.

CHAPTER **18**

✦Carving Out a
Place for
Volunteers

*O*N a cold, clear February morning, the chapel
at Focus on the Family's Colorado Springs headquarters
filled with employees and volunteers for the observance of
Volunteer Day. After a rousing songfest, a select group of
volunteers marched across the platform to receive recog-
nition for their service. Among those honored was Tom
Drennon, who had logged a total of six thousand volunteer hours. Tom and his wife, Merle, hold a unique place
among volunteers at Focus on the Family in that they are
generally known as the couple who influenced Focus to
launch its volunteer program.

After Tom spent thirty-one years as a postman in
Sacramento, California, the Drennons began to look for a
new place to live and a place to do volunteer work. They
dreamed about Colorado, with its massive mountains and
changing seasons—a pleasant change from the long, hot
summers of the Sacramento valley. And the Colorado
Springs–based Focus on the Family organization seemed
a perfect place to serve as volunteers. They forged ahead
with what looked to be a good plan. But their letter of
inquiry to Focus on the Family brought a disappointing
response: The organization had no volunteer program.

The initial negative response might have ended the

SAGE ADVICE

✦✦✦✦✦

*P*ray, be open, and look. We are living proof that if you want to do something, you need to start looking.

TOM AND MERLE DRENNON

matter for the Drennons had it not been for a subsequent Colorado vacation and a visit to Focus on the Family headquarters. While there, Tom and Merle had a chance encounter at the elevator with Dr. Dobson. He engaged them in friendly conversation and in the process made a startling suggestion: "You ought to come here and work with us."

"We would," Merle replied with enthusiasm, "but you have no volunteer program." But Dr. Dobson persisted. He urged them to contact Mark Maddox before they left the building. The Drennons followed his advice, and from that point on things moved very quickly. In fact, by the time Tom and Merle came on board there were already seventy-eight volunteers in the program.

Shortly after their visit, the Drennons were notified that the volunteer program had been established and that there would be a place for them whenever they were ready. Since their Sacramento house had been on the market for a year, neither Tom nor Merle was very optimistic about moving anytime soon. To take the edge off their disappointment, they planned a trip to the Springs to coincide with the dedication of the administration and operations buildings at Focus on the Family. But when a buyer suddenly appeared, requesting occupancy of their house in thirty days, the Drennons hurriedly upgraded their planned trip from "vacation" to "relocation." Arriving in the Springs two days before the planned dedication, they found a motel and called Focus headquarters. "When do you want us to come to work?" they asked.

"Tomorrow," came the reply.

Almost a decade later, Tom and Merle still look back on their move to Colorado Springs as a "God thing." With barely time to unpack their suitcases, they took on their first assignment—setting up chairs for the dedication. They served as greeters on the day the new buildings opened.

When they arrived at Focus, the Drennons were asked how much time they wanted to give. They committed themselves to "four hours a day or whenever we are needed." In the spirit of true volunteerism, they offered to do "whatever needs to be done." Frequently Merle is needed for her computer skills. She also works in shipping and packing for mailing. Tom's six thousand hours, which began with setting up chairs, have encompassed everything from packing books to giving tours to acting as host at the welcome center.

The Drennons' involvement with the volunteer program doesn't end at the door to Focus headquarters. They frequently act as host and hostess for new volunteers. Some will stay with Tom and Merle as they look for a home; others will stay with them as they come to the Springs for a short-term volunteer job.

At the present time for a variety of personal reasons the Drennons are anticipating a return to California. But they do not anticipate an end to volunteer work. They came to Colorado Springs because it gave them an opportunity to serve the Lord. They believe that God will continue to give them opportunities so long as they continue to tell Him, "We'll do whatever you want, whenever you need us."

Contacts:

Focus on the Family Volunteers
(800) 531-1626
www.family.org/volunteers/
E-mail: volunteer@fotf.org

CHAPTER **19**

◆ Thursdays with Evon

*E*VON HEDLEY has been a friend and colleague of mine for more than fifty years. We first met when we both were active in Youth for Christ. When I later became president of the organization, I invited him to be our executive director. In addition, his wife, Jean, is my wife, Dorothy's, closest friend.

Once a month Evon steps out of his apartment on Orange Grove Boulevard in Pasadena, California, to a waiting car that whisks him off to CoCo's, where he and the driver enjoy one of the full breakfast specials. Evon likes the eggs with bacon or sausage and hash browns. But it's not the breakfast that brings him to this place. His driver, who always stands on the passenger side of the car and holds the door open for Evon, is not a chauffeur. He is a young man whom Evon is mentoring.

At eighty-five, Evon Hedley speaks with a strong voice that belies his age. He considers himself in good health and declares that mentoring younger men keeps his perspective youthful.

"I tell the ones I meet with today that the only difference between them and me is that I'm down the road further. I know where the potholes are and the hairpin curves and the speed bumps." He believes that being

SAGE ADVICE

◆◆◆◆◆

If you want to mentor, Romans 12:8 is a great verse for you. The verse speaks of the gift of encouragement, and mentoring is encouraging.

EVON HEDLEY

down the road further makes it important for him to share what he's discovered so that the young men can avoid some of the same hazards.

While his interest in young men goes back to his own younger days working with Youth for Christ, his mentoring ministry became more fully defined during his final career position as a vice president at World Vision. The younger men on staff often approached him for lunch sessions. Sometimes Evon approached them. As they discussed all aspects of life, including but not limited to spiritual issues, Evon began to define what mentoring is not. "It is not a Bible study, not a prayer meeting, not discipling. It is helping to bring balance into the life of the person being mentored."

Most of the young men with whom Evon meets are the beneficiaries of education far beyond what he has. But they seek him out to learn about the lessons of life. They are looking for balance in their lives, and Evon seeks to encourage them in their pursuit.

Since leaving World Vision about a dozen years ago, Evon has had the opportunity to meet with younger men in various businesses and professions, including some theology students. While not a seminary graduate himself, he mentored a young student from nearby Fuller Seminary for five years. They met once a week until the student completed his Ph.D. in psychology. During one critical period the student had a number of theological questions for which Evon had no answers. But he provided a needed sounding board which, in time, helped the student find his own answers.

As a key to effective mentoring, Evon always focuses on the relationship itself. From the start, he seeks to build a relationship in which young men can be confident and secure enough to bare their souls. "When that happens," Evon says, "the mentor is able to help the one being mentored."

Evon encourages mentorees to set their own agendas. They can talk about anything they choose, and he encourages practical questions. A healthy octogenarian, he has earned the right to remind them that the body is the temple of the Holy Spirit and needs to be taken care of. With single young men he especially likes to find out about their eating habits, if they are having regular check-ups with the doctor and dentist, and if they get proper sleep and take regular vacations. He maintains that the physical affects the spiritual, the social, and the career issues of life. He describes the process as a domino effect moving through all areas of life.

Evon always encourages his mentorees to talk about relationships with the opposite sex, married relationships, sex itself, pornography, and other related subjects. He has discovered that these are important issues for most young men, yet few have trusted confidants with whom to discuss their concerns.

Whatever the subject, Evon has one purpose in his mentoring sessions. The thrust of each meeting is the "application of biblical truth as I bring suggestions and answers to their lives." This is what Thursdays (or Mondays or Tuesdays) with Evon are all about.

CHAPTER **20**

✦Finding Life beyond Happy Trails

*G*OLF LOVERS and sun worshipers find Happy Trails Resort in Surprise, Arizona, a dream come true. Palm trees wave near the guardhouse, where visitors are handed a map to guide them through the maze of mobile homes that are uniquely positioned beside and between the eighteen holes of the golf course.

Ruth Crew lives at the fourteenth hole. To reach her house you drive on Happy Trails Street, past Trigger and Dale Evans Drive. A right turn at Roy Rogers Street, a left at Nelly Belle, and some circling and searching brings you to the right number on Blacksmith. Inside, through the dining room plate-glass windows, the fourteenth hole comes into view. Two women, barely forty feet away, swing their clubs.

For Ruth, golfing and sun are not the vital ingredients for life after seventy. She recalls that when she and her late husband moved to Surprise's Happy Trails Resort in 1991, they joined in many activities and the church that meets in the resort ballroom. But she found something lacking.

"You can come to a place like Happy Trails and find lots of activities," she said. "It's fun but it's temporary. The real thing that satisfies is when you do something for the Lord and He blesses it."

SAGE ADVICE

✦✦✦✦✦

Anybody can do volunteer work. It's the most wonderful, exciting thing you can do. You meet people and you are of service to them, and it's the most satisfying thing you can do.

RUTH CREW

Feeling that a life focused inward was not the way she wanted to live out her senior years, Ruth began to look for something more. Today her "happy trails" are apt to lead to Boulder City, to Ohio, to Missouri—anywhere she can find a need and fill it.

Ruth belongs to a volunteer group called SOWER—an anagram for Servants On Wheels Ever Ready. With sparkling eyes and a ready smile, she explains that she leaves in less than twenty-four hours for her next assignment.

Since joining SOWER, Ruth and her work partner, Mary, have done everything from stuffing envelopes to pulling weeds. One day might find them cleaning the inside of a house. The next day they are painting the exterior. At Boulder City, in a home for children who have been abused, Ruth did correspondence and general office work.

Her first project as a SOWER was a stint at King's Domain, the Ohio offices of Athletes in Action. "We did everything," she explains. "We cooked. We painted buildings. We worked in the yard. We did office work." She worked a total of four months at King's Domain.

Her next assignment takes her to Child Evangelism Fellowship offices in Warrenton, Missouri, where she will assist in the correspondence course ministry. CEF has a correspondence course that reaches all over the world to children, adults, and inmates in jails. Ruth's job will be to grade the returned coursework, write a note to the student, and pray specifically for that person.

Unlike volunteers with similar organizations, SOWER workers do not always travel and live in motor homes. In Warrenton, Ruth and Mary will live in accommodations provided on the premises. SOWER also differs in that it accepts single women volunteers.

Ruth learned about SOWER from Mary, a casual acquaintance who approached her after church one Sunday night. Mary asked her if she would consider becoming a SOWER, gave her some literature, and said, "I'd like you to be my partner. My children don't like me to travel alone."

Ruth admits that her penchant for adventure may have drawn her to SOWER. (The year she turned seventy she motorbiked across Europe with a nephew.) But she recalls that she learned of the organization at a time when she was seeking God's direction for her future. When Mary approached her, Ruth, by then a widow, was thinking of making a change. Convinced that Mary was God's messenger, Ruth agreed to become a SOWER.

Today she sings the praises of SOWER to anyone who will listen. "It's an ideal setup for people who have quit work," she says. Tomorrow she will put her words into action. Once more she will leave Roy Rogers Street and Dale Evans Drive behind and go in search of other happy trails.

Contacts

SOWER Ministry
14771 CR 424
Lindale, TX 75771
(903) 882-8070
E-mail: Soweroffice@juno.com

CHAPTER **21**

✦ The Biggest
Challenges Come
after Seventy

WHEN Ann Smith takes her place behind the
pulpit of the Park Place Church of God in Anderson,
Indiana, she looks out over the cross-shaped sanctuary
and sees a congregation sprinkled with retired ministers,
university professors, seminary professors, retired deans,
and one or two past presidents of Anderson University.
Located on the campus of the university, Park Place
Church would be a formidable challenge to any pastor.
For Ann, the unexpected call to become interim pastor of
her home church led to the most challenging position of
her career.

For nine years prior to the call Ann traveled about the
country speaking at state conventions, ministers' meetings, and church retreats. At age seventy-five, she looked
at her speaking schedule, considered the toll it was taking
on her and her ailing husband, and decided to quit traveling. "I thought I was clearing my schedule so that I could
be home with Nathan," she recalls, "but God had other
plans." Shortly after she completed all her engagements,
she received the call from Park Place.

Ann's first response to the committee was, "Why me?"
As they began to talk more seriously about it, she told
them, "There are two things you need to understand.

> ## SAGE ADVICE
> ✦✦✦✦✦
>
> **W**e need to constantly rediscover: rediscover the joy of living, rediscover the beauty of the world, rediscover relationships, rediscover everything in life.
>
> ANN SMITH

One, I am seventy-five years old, and two, if Nathan needs me, that's where I will be. He comes ahead of everything." The committee assured her they could live with both conditions.

Nathan has had multiple myeloma for fourteen years. Living with cancer has brought changes for the Smiths, but they have never allowed it to become the focus of their lives.

Nathan encouraged Ann to accept the committee's invitation. "I am married to a man who encourages me constantly to try something different and new," she explains. She reasoned that the position would allow her to stay home but still be involved in ministry. The very fact that she had cleared her calendar before the pulpit committee called seemed significant. "Nobody thought I would [quit traveling] and yet I did. So I said, 'God, are you saying something to me?'"

As interim pastor of the approximately six hundred-member congregation, Ann plunged into a routine of board meetings, committees, staff sessions, planning services, sermon preparation, hospital calls, and counseling. She admits that, although not intimidated by the makeup of the congregation, she might not have had the courage to become their pastor twenty years ago. She credits age and experience with preparing her for the challenges she faces at Park Place.

Meeting life's challenges began early for Ann. At age sixteen she went to work in the steel mills of Alabama because her father died and the family needed the income. Later, with her mother's encouragement, Ann went to Indiana to seek further education at Anderson College (now Anderson University). She showed up on the doorstep one day and said, "More than anything else I want to go to school." She had no high school diploma, but after three days of tests the college admitted her. She subsequently earned both her bachelor's and master's degrees.

While at Anderson, she met and married Nathan, a young widower, with whom she spent thirty years ministering in Japan. They came home from Japan for Ann to become the Asia administrator for their mission board. After five years Ann took a position with the university as director of church relations. During her tenure there, Nathan's disease was diagnosed.

Living with cancer has been a personal challenge to both Ann and Nathan. (They are quick to distinguish between living with cancer and dying with cancer.) The prognosis of Nathan's disease pointed to a few remaining years. "People don't live for fourteen years with multiple myeloma," Ann says. "Four years is considered to be a long time to live with the disease." Others might have decided to drop everything, stay at home, and spend the time together, but the Smiths, after much consideration, determined that Ann should continue to do what she had been doing.

Nathan believes that Ann's involvement outside the home brings balance to their lives. They can talk about the day's events and pray about whatever problems arise.

Ann's realistic view of life in general allows her to enjoy life after seventy with whatever challenges it brings.

She recognizes that every age has its trials as well as its blessings. But she cautions seniors to focus not on what is lost but on what is left.

On her seventieth birthday, Ann celebrated for a month by writing "lessons learned" on three by five cards. On her first card she wrote *God is committed to Ann Smith.* "All my life I heard sermons about how I needed to be committed to God," she explains, "but I never heard any on how God is committed to me. As I reflected on seventy years of living, the most outstanding thing that came through is that God is committed to me. He never gives up. I would have given up on me years ago."

She credits her mother with teaching her to view every period of life as "the best years of your life." By way of explanation, Ann adds, "Every age is the best because it prepares you for the next." In a recent sermon at Park Place Church, Ann made the point, "I am seventy-six. I cannot change the age I am, nor do I want to. Every age is the best yet."

She acknowledges that in her seventies she has faced her two biggest challenges—caring for Nathan and pastoring Park Place Church. But she hasn't done it alone. God is still committed to Ann Smith.

CHAPTER 22

✦ Three Men
on a Mission:
Bob Ancha

*F*ROM his office in bustling midtown Chicago, Bob Ancha spent most of his working years running the company he founded, Ancha Electronic, Inc. Today he is more likely to be found in a teeming central market of Ghana where merchants, without benefit of offices, conduct their business. In Chicago he fought traffic jams or rode the El. In Ghana he picks his way along open sewer areas and narrow passages where locals produce and sell their wares. Leather merchants make and sell shoes, purses, and wallets. Others walk about with moving stores on their heads: baskets of produce, clothing, batteries, or live chickens. Away from the crowded market Bob walks along dirt roads where furniture makers and auto mechanics have set up open-air shops. He may look like any other American tourist, but wherever he goes, Bob Ancha is a man with a mission. He is in Ghana to teach impoverished people to become self-sufficient.

Bob believes that the difference between charity and philanthropy is the difference between giving a man a fish and teaching a man to fish. For a decade he made charitable donations through the Robert A. Ancha Family Foundation. One trip to Ghana convinced him that he should

SAGE ADVICE

✦✦✦✦✦

I wish I would have started earlier. Ours was a small company and we didn't receive a lot of money for it. People who are more successful could perhaps sell their businesses earlier and get involved in missions or evangelism or whatever the Lord has laid on their hearts incidental to their gifts.

BOB ANCHA

move beyond charitable giving to action that would have lasting benefits for the recipients.

He describes his first experience in Ghana as enlightening but unfulfilling. He saw needs that he endeavored to meet through charitable gifts. But he had reservations about encouraging Ghanaian people to become dependent on others.

After returning home he began to meditate on two scriptures: 1 Thessalonians 4:11-12 and 1 Timothy 5:8. The first extols working with our hands so that we win the respect of outsiders, not depending on others. The second declares that if anyone does not provide for his own, he has denied the faith and is worse than an unbeliever. Ancha determined that when he returned to Ghana it would be to help the people provide for themselves—to become self-sufficient.

On his next trip to Ghana he focused on Ghanaian women who needed loans to establish or enlarge their own business. He set up a program for funding the women with micro-loans that would be repaid in time.

To carry out his purpose, Bob works in conjunction with the 1,800-member Tafo Church in Kumasi. Twenty-five women merchants from the church received the first series of loans. To qualify for the loan, each woman was required to attend an eight-week training session. In a further effort to ensure accountability, the women are required to assume corporate responsibility for any defaulted loans within the group. Bob emphasizes that the women are not being handed money to help in their business; they are given a loan and they are being trained to be good businesswomen. Using his expertise to assist, train, and encourage the women merchants, he sees himself as an entrepreneur helping other entrepreneurs.

That he is an entrepreneur, there can be no doubt. When as a young man he founded Ancha Electronic, Inc., he was an engineer with no expertise in business. He loved the hands-on part—installing sound systems in churches, stadiums, and airports—but he needed help to become a responsible businessman. He set out to learn everything about small business practices by attending college-level seminars on the subject. The business grew to over one hundred employees with offices in five cities throughout the United States, including Honolulu. Bob describes his business as a company that God led him to start and a company built by God.

After one of the many business seminars he attended, Bob decided to establish the family foundation from which he makes charitable donations. Through careful investment of the original eighty thousand dollars, the fund has increased to over a million dollars, allowing him to contribute some fifty or sixty thousand dollars annually to missionary causes around the world.

Throughout his years as head of the electronics company, Bob made it a practice to arrive at his office at 6:00 A.M. to have a quiet time in the Word and pray for God to show him what to do for the day. At age sixty-four in one of his early-morning sessions with God, he had his first thoughts about selling the business. From nowhere a question suddenly came to him: "Why don't you retire, Bob?" He looked around to see if anyone was in the room. Convinced that it was God's message to him, Bob began to take the necessary steps to turn over the leadership of the company to someone else.

In May 1998 he went with three other men from the Chicago area to Ghana. All entrepreneurs, they offered some leadership training and contributed money to a few needy causes. Bob remembers the experience left him unsatisfied because it was too much like giving fish where the real need was to teach people how to fish. By the time he returned to Ghana two years later, he had a plan in place. His "training men to fish" program became a "training women in business" program.

Before his return trip to Ghana, the Anchas moved to Prescott, Arizona, to be near their daughter. In Prescott, he recruited two other men to join him—Peter Grey and Dr. Charlie Bahn, whose stories are told in the next two chapters. (A fourth man from Chicago also went.)

Between trips to Ghana, Bob Ancha is very active in his local church. "We are busier than we ever were," he declares. He is thrilled about every opportunity to minis-ter. ("Thrill" is a word that he uses often.) But working with Ghanaian merchants is the topic that always brings a glint to his eyes and excitement to his voice. For a seasoned entrepreneur there is nothing more thrilling than assisting Third World entrepreneurs.

CHAPTER **23**

✦ Three Men
on a Mission:
Peter Grey

*T*HE CITY OF Prescott, Arizona's first capital, is
one of several mile-high cities in the state and is much
cooler than Phoenix, the present-day capital. Yavapai
County offices are located in the center of old Prescott in
a typical vintage courthouse building. A columned struc-
ture with many steps leading to its entrance, it sits in the
middle of a block-square park and is surrounded by stat-
ues. Across the street another vintage building, now listed
on the historic register, houses the ministries of First
Baptist Church. Its seven hundred-plus membership is a
pleasant blend of pioneer families and recent transplants.
Among the transplants is Peter Grey, a Britisher who
came to the U.S. by way of Canada, spent most of his life
in the East, and, after much research, settled upon
Prescott as the place to spend his senior years.

"It was a no-brainer as to which church we would affili-
ate with when we came here," Peter says. Visiting the
church had been part of a "research" trip prior to their
move. On that trip Peter and his wife, Doris, met a British
couple from Zimbabwe who invited the Greys to visit
their growth group. In the intervening years before the
Greys moved West, the two couples kept in touch.

A chemist now in his sixties, Peter has been retired

SAGE ADVICE

✦✦✦✦

You need to give of yourself. Keep your mind active as a retiree.

PETER GREY

from Mobile Research and Development Corporation since 1996. Currently he is a management consultant working about half-time. This job takes him away from home an average of two weeks out of the month, but at times it stretches to three or four weeks.

Still, the Greys find time to be involved in their church. Doris works with the Stephen Ministry. Peter is writing a new missions policy, leading a growth group, and waiting to hear what needs to be done for a church in Ghana that he visited a year ago.

Peter was a last-minute addition to the team that went to Ghana with Bob Ancha (see page 93) last year. He laughs easily over how the trip came about. Originally he explored the idea of going to Ghana on safari but could find no one to go with him. Bob Ancha half-jokingly said, "If you can't go on safari, go with us on our mission trip." Peter was willing but had already booked a consulting job that conflicted with the dates. When the consulting job was canceled unexpectedly, he said, "Well, God, I guess I'm going to Ghana."

For Peter, it was a vision trip. A trip to discover what could be done. Finding that much of Ghana is openly Christian was a surprise to him, and he sees that as a logical platform on which to build. He describes the local church with which the team worked as "very big but dirt poor—without resources and unable to get resources in their own country." Just twenty miles from the megachurch is a village that is largely untouched by Christianity. While the church has a vision for the neighboring community, they can do little about it because they are struggling to keep things together in their own congregation.

As one who has been involved in missions programs for fifteen years, Peter firmly believes that a "vision" trip changes the way people respond to missions. Raised in a denomination that supported missions but never had personal contact with missionaries, he came late in life to a New Jersey church that drastically changed his own response. The church urged its members to participate in short mission trips, and Peter got involved, eventually organizing several trips to various countries. It was there that he caught a vision for missions.

His management skills and his past experience make him a logical choice to organize the next trip to Ghana with Bob Ancha. In preparation for the return trip this fall, Peter studies the known needs and considers how to best meet those needs. He would like to see the city church reach out to the neighboring village through children's Bible school and some adult meetings. For the city church, Peter sees both immediate and long-term goals. For now the pressing need is to assist the women in developing their ministries and to help establish an Awana program. Eventually the school run by the church will need help in construction.

He also has stated goals for the team itself, including the addition of several high school students. Every team member will raise his or her own funding and commit to a period of training. As part of their training, team members will prepare a testimony and practice giving it in a simulated translation setting. In addition to the obvious practical benefits of these requirements, Grey emphasizes that through personal fund-raising, members recruit prayer partners. Through training together, the group melds as a team.

Working part-time, serving his church, and organizing a team to assist a poor church in Ghana are a few of the things that keep purpose alive for Peter Grey. But he believes there are many ways to accomplish that. "If anyone in retirement years came to me and said, 'I don't know what to do,' I'd have a hard time restraining myself," he says. "Opportunities are vast."

CHAPTER **24**

✦Three Men
on a Mission:
Dr. Charles Bahn

SILVER-HAIRED, seventy-three-year-old Dr.
Charles Bahn exercises regularly: tennis two or three times
a week, skiing several times a year. It shows. Slim and trim,
dressed in blue jeans, a turtleneck shirt, and comfortable
boat shoes, he is a bit late for an appointment because he
has been test-driving a new eight-passenger Dodge
Durango. A midwesterner transplanted to Arizona, he
contemplates using the van to visit nine grandchildren
scattered over Indiana, Tennessee, and California.

Dr. Bahn no longer practices as a gastroenterologist, but
he still works as an expert witness for the court system for
disability determination denials. These days he gives more
time to hobbies developed over the years. In his Prescott
home he turns out bowls with turquoise inlay, which are
sold through galleries in nearby Sedona. His wife is an
award-winning artist who works in oils. Both are active in
the First Baptist Church of Prescott, Arizona.

Charlie, as he is known by his friends, was the third
member of the team led by Bob Ancha on the mission
trip to Ghana (see page 93), for which he describes his
qualifications as "98 percent retired physician, shoeshine
boy, and luggage carrier for the trip."

Charlie's many years as a committed Christian add a

SAGE ADVICE

✦✦✦✦✦

We need help in Ghana both in the business world and in the field of medicine. We can't bring about change overnight, but it can happen. We have a saying, "Anyone can eat an elephant, but only if you take one bite at a time." If we start today we can make things better tomorrow.

DR. CHARLES BAHN

spiritual dimension to his qualifications. He credits medical school with opening his eyes to what a great and wonderful God must have created us. His faith awakened as he saw the wonders of the human body: the blood supply, the nerve connections, the muscles, and the brain, which he notes still functions one hundred times faster than the fastest computer. While in medical school he attended a Bible study led by a doctor friend, which furthered his interest in Christianity. In time a more active faith took deep root and became a priority.

In between "shining shoes and carrying luggage" in Ghana, Charlie set up shop under some cashew trees and examined twenty or thirty plantation workers and their wives. To reach the cashew farm, the group drove into the jungle to the end of a road, then walked the rest of the way. A bit wary, Charlie asked whether there were snakes.

"Oh, we have pythons here."

"Any others?"

"Cobras."

"And others?"

"Yes, there are poisonous ones but I don't know their name."

Charlie emphasizes that he stuck close to the path for the last three-fourths of a mile.

At the impromptu "cashew clinic" the team distributed about 250 pieces of children's clothing they had brought along. Workers helped carry in the suitcases containing the clothing. After the team laid all the items on the ground, the workers and wives made the rounds, picking up two pieces at a time, then continuing to circle until the clothing was gone.

In Kumasi, a city of 1.2 million people, Charlie took note of the many signs that speak of the missionary influence of the past one hundred years. A sampling: "Jesus Power Electric Co.," "Remember God Radiator Shop," "Not I but Christ Taxi," and, for the ladies, "Praise the Lord Beauty Salon." Thousands of similar signs can be seen on almost every block of both the capital city of Accra and of Kumasi, the second-largest city in Ghana. But Bahn also took note of the fact that the missionary influence ended about halfway to the back country. From that point on there are many opportunities for evangelism.

The primary reason for going to Ghana was to encourage the 1,800-member Tafo Baptist Church of Kumasi and to partner with them in ongoing ministry efforts. Charlie confesses to feeling confused initially by many things in the country, but a commitment to the task and a brief adjustment period helped him feel at ease with the Ghanaians.

As he became more aware of their needs he added new, medically related goals to the existing team goals. Through the eyes of a physician he saw a need for more medical care: a need to get rid of polio, malaria, AIDS, typhoid, and cholera; a need to help train more doctors and improve their skills. He met with university hospital doctors in Ghana to discover their specific needs in the area of training, equipment, and supplies. He also discovered current personnel needs in ophthalmology, in general surgery, and in orthopedic surgery. As he looks to the future he envisions both businessmen and physicians from the U.S. coming to Ghana to address these challenges.

Charlie Bahn knows that his church will have a continuing relationship with the Kumasi church. As another team prepares to go this fall, he contemplates whether or not to revisit Ghana this year. If he goes, he is determined to find other doctors to go along.

He knows the need. Now he only has to find some able senior physicians who are willing to walk a path where cobras lurk, and, if necessary, open a practice under some cashew trees.

CHAPTER **25**

✦Freely Received,
Freely Giving

*S*EVENTY-SEVEN-year-old Nancy Bayless
learned the value of mentoring at a very early age from
her grandfather. In one of her many published magazine
articles she writes of his influence on her life. Using
powerful images, she shows how a retired judge mentored
his beloved grandchild even from his deathbed. "I left
childhood behind that day," she writes. "I realized for the
first time how powerful one life can be as it touches other
lives."

Sixty-seven years later, Nancy is quietly touching the
lives of others as she mentors women through her church
and aspiring writers through her local writers' guild.

For twenty-five years Nancy lived on a series of boats
in various Southern California harbors. Four years ago she
gave up the blue waters of the Pacific for a small apartment in San Diego located just three blocks from her
church. She is actively involved in the congregation's
ministry—from small group Bible studies, to editing and
writing the church newsletter, to counseling and
mentoring.

Of her mentoring she explains that she sees herself as
the broad-shouldered church grandma. Sometimes acting
as a sounding board, sometimes giving needed counsel,

SAGE ADVICE

✦✦✦✦✦

*F*irst, know that God is in control. Let Him be your best friend and pray for his will. Then have a good attitude. Don't complain about your ills. Keep a positive attitude and live one day at a time.

NANCY BAYLESS

she regularly spends time with younger women. Some are assigned to her through the church counseling program. Over a year ago her pastor asked her to work with a young girl. "I mentor her all the time," Nancy says. In fact, the girl, who is soon to be married, has lived with Nancy for six months.

Combining her writing skills with her counseling, Nancy has written a study on the value of touching, which she is currently teaching once a week to two different groups. The subject is one of Nancy's passions. She has been known to walk up to hand-holding married couples and say, "Don't ever stop."

In part, Nancy's teaching on touching derived from her widowhood. She confesses that after her husband died the thing she missed the most was touching. But Nancy also sees touching as something important to people in their senior years. She believes that when older people see their spouses or friends die, they need close friends who will touch them.

Mentoring writers is Nancy's other great passion. "We [writers] all had help and I want to give it back," she says. A lifelong writer who has only published in the past dozen years, Nancy credits best-selling author Jerry Jenkins with mentoring her. "I got wonderful rejection letters," she says, "but nothing sold until I met Jerry."

Friends for over a decade, Nancy recalls their first meeting at a Point Loma Christian Writers' Guild conference. During a fifteen-minute appointment, Jenkins picked up her writing sample, looked at it for about five seconds, and asked, "May I take this home?" The next day he asked her to write her testimony and send it to him at *Moody* magazine. Stunned at the request, Nancy realized for the first time how much it meant to her to be a writer.

The mentoring process began when Jerry wrote on a sheet of paper, "Nancy you're a wonderful writer—not perfect, but wonderful." After she sent her testimony to him, Jerry returned it filled with blue-pencil corrections. He cautioned her that her budding career as a writer depended on how she accepted suggestions and criticism. While the article was eventually published, it did not happen until the editor to whom Jerry directed the piece asked Nancy to rewrite it five times. Although "bummed out," Nancy recognized the truth of Jerry's words and learned to accept both suggestions and criticism.

Today she gives suggestions and criticism to other writers and to nonwriting young women in budding careers or troubled marriages. She has learned by example that the best mentoring is accomplished through honest communication. What she has freely received, she now is freely giving.

CHAPTER **26**

✦Making Plans,
Discovering
Directions

*A*T 9 P.M. on a cold, foggy, February night,
Dick and Lynn Korthals leave the comfort of their fire-
place to pick up a stranger at the Colorado Springs
airport. Lynn waits in the car in the loading zone while
Dick goes to the gate one more time to check on the now
five-hours-late passenger. The passenger is a guest of
Focus on the Family—in town for a business consulta-
tion—and meeting her is but one of many duties Dick
and Lynn perform for the Focus ministries. By the time
the Korthals deposit their passenger at the motel it is past
bedtime for this late-seventies couple. But early tomorrow
morning they will both be at Focus headquarters filling in
wherever needed.

The Korthals' home sits on the highest point of Inspiration Drive on the crest of a ridge. The master bedroom is
located on the top level of the quad-level house. Most
mornings Dick pads his way through the French doors leading from the bedroom through his twelve foot by twenty
foot office to the balcony. He describes his first view every
morning as "the wonders of God's creation." His first
thought is one of thanksgiving for his volunteer work. "I
wake up every morning thinking I have something to do,"

SAGE ADVICE

Keep your mind open and your spirit willing. God puts opportunities before you.

DICK AND LYNN
KORTHALS

he says. "I hate to think of life without Focus on the Family."

Seven years ago, out of curiosity, the Korthals toured the Focus campus with a church group. On the way out they heard someone say, "We need volunteers." Both Dick and Lynn picked up applications, and within a week they were interviewed. To date Dick has chalked up in excess of 4,500 volunteer hours with the organization and Lynn has accumulated 3,000 hours.

Dick credits the air force with allowing him to give his time to volunteer work. "The one great thing the air force gave me was enough income so that I could do volunteer work."

Well, not quite. In a sense the air force also gave him his wife, whom he describes as "very devoted and willing to go along with all my whims and ways, never complaining about my decisions."

During World War II, Lynn was an air-vac nurse and Dick was a troop carrier pilot in the Philippines. After flying together once they decided to spend the rest of their lives together. They set a wedding date, never dreaming that it would coincide with the day the war ended—August 15, 1945.

The one great principle Dick has learned is that man makes plans, but God directs his steps. Over the years he pushed at doors, tried different careers, and anticipated earning degrees in several fields, including theology. But at each juncture, often at the last minute, God closed the door and thrust him into a divinely appointed opportunity.

His background in computers prepared him for essential volunteer work at Focus. His background in public speaking, forced upon him when he felt very inadequate for the task, prepared him for the weekend pulpit supply that he does in the many small churches in their area. His theological training, although interrupted, has given him a solid foundation for this as well.

Dick also serves as treasurer and chaplain for the Pilot Class 43-D Association, a nonprofit organization of the surviving members of the Army Air Corps flying class that graduated in April 1943. (This is the largest class of pilots ever to graduate.)

Prior to working at Focus on the Family, the Korthals did volunteer work in other areas. Lynn began volunteering at a Ronald MacDonald house where parents stay to be near their severely ill, hospitalized children. She continues with this one day a month.

Dick credits his interest in volunteering to the first Sunday school class he was asked to teach. "I found it such a joy, I sought opportunities to volunteer after that."

Dick admits that not all volunteer positions are the same. And one's background can define the unpleasant opportunities as well as the pleasant ones. For three years he volunteered several times a week as a docent with the park system, taking kids on nature walks. But as a man who had written a paper on "The Role of Religion in the Space Age," defending the Genesis account of Creation, he found it frustrating not to be allowed to mention his belief.

At Focus on the Family, Lynn works with the radio ministry doing filing, correspondence, invoices, and writing checks to the radio stations each month. Dick has done many jobs, beginning with lining up speakers and doing publicity for a weekly noon employee's forum. He spent a year computerizing the library so that now a volunteer can step in for a day at a time and manage it. He also wrote a manual for the librarians. Currently he is working on the computers at the "Focus Over 50" department.

Speaking for both of them, Dick says, "I think working at Focus has added years and years to our life. It gives us purpose."

CHAPTER **27**

✦Doing What He
Loves to Do

*T*HE FIRST THING Edd Brown tells you about
his spacious split-level cedar log home is that it was built
by volunteers, which seems appropriate since Edd has
spent a lifetime directing volunteer efforts. The large
dining-room windows provide a clear view of the heavily
forested canyon that abuts their property. At the edge of
the wraparound deck a red-trunked madrone tree stretches
toward the sky. Edd leads a tour through the lower level
of the house, ending in his office. This is where he often
begins the day when he isn't trotting the globe.

A large world map, strategically placed above Edd's
desk, allows him to track his past volunteer efforts.
Colored pins are scattered across several continents,
marking the places where Edd has directed those efforts.
"It began as disaster relief," he explains, pointing to a pin
in Central America.

Specifically, it began with an earthquake in Guatemala. Edd had recently accepted a new position with his
denomination in which he would train volunteers for
missions projects around the world. When the call came
from Guatemala, Edd plunged into his first attempt at
disaster relief.

"We've had an earthquake," the caller said. "Here's

SAGE ADVICE

❖❖❖❖❖

Everybody has something that grabs them. There is something inside of everyone that they really want to focus on . . . maybe family, travel, or whatever. My advice is to take that and build on it but don't build selfishly. The worst thing in the world that a person can do, physically, mentally, or spiritually, is to start focusing internally.

EDD BROWN

what we would like you to get." Edd called on friends in three counties of the San Francisco Bay area and put together a team of doctors to go to Guatemala.

The flood at Utah's Teton Dam was the next disaster to which Edd sent volunteers. He coordinated about 150 people to work in the area for six months. He looks back upon Guatemala and Utah as the two events that solidified the volunteer program. What began as disaster relief quickly developed into other volunteer efforts. "Volunteerism was just beginning," he recalls. "We began building schools and churches and helping people in small businesses." The program met immediate needs and it served as a training ground for people involved in disaster relief. During his career, Edd saw in excess of five thousand people serving as volunteers.

Officially "retired" for nearly a decade, Edd has seen little change in his schedule. He describes the biggest difference between now and then as doing the same thing for a different reason. "I'm not doing it because I'm supposed to do it. I always loved my work, but I did it because it was my job. Now I do it just for the fun of it."

Not all the pins on Edd's map are from the years when he loved his work but did it because it was his job. He has continued to add pins since he began doing the same thing just because he loves to do it. He points to a pin in Turkey where he supervised the rebuilding of a village destroyed by an earthquake. Another pin marks Jerusalem, where he helped rebuild a Baptist church that had been firebombed. There are pins to mark recent volunteer efforts in Russia. This year the volunteers he coordinates will complete their sixth church building in Russia.

His early life as a pastor prepared Edd for the work he would do as a globe-circling builder. In every church he pastored he became involved in an expansion program and directed whatever enlargement or building program was being done. Later he worked with his denomination at the state level in a program that assisted small churches in outlying areas. The state organization underwrote his training and testing to become a licensed contractor. This enabled Edd to go into churches with few resources and serve as their contractor. Later, in the overseas projects, he found it easy to work with the building departments.

Diversity has marked Edd's volunteer efforts in his post-retirement years. Calling upon his past experience as a pastor, he taught in Russia in a series of training schools for young men and women who want to become leaders and pastors. He also served as interim pastor in Swangford, Germany, and in Munich.

If an official "retirement" did nothing to change his schedule, it did help him and his wife, Flo, acquire the house of their dreams. At a retirement party hosted by his friends, a miniature log house was constructed as part of the decor. The emcee explained for those who had not already heard that Edd was planning to build a log house in Amador County. "If you hire anyone to work on it, we will never speak to you again," he threatened. Edd waves his hands over the room. "This is the house that volunteers built."

He'll be sleeping at home more often this year since he has no overseas trips planned. But he will be busy nevertheless. "I've let eight small churches along Highway 49 talk me into working with them as director of missions. I'll be counseling, helping train pastors, helping to develop mission programs, just doing whatever I can to assist these eight congregations." Perhaps next year will take him overseas again. In either place, here or there, Edd Brown is moving through the latter years of his life doing what he loves to do.

CHAPTER **28**
✦ Using Music as an Entrance into Hearts

*I*T'S Friday night, and Tucson, Arizona, residents Jim and Celia Huckabay are loading their multiple instruments into their aging Dodge for a weekly jam session at the Country Gospel Jamboree. A short drive brings them to a gutted-out mobile home turned auditorium for one hundred. Once there, they have only to decide which will be their instrument of choice for the first number. Celia plays piano, accordion, and harmonica. Jim plays violin and guitar, but those who understand the difference will tell you that Jim actually plays three instruments because he does equally well on violin or fiddle. Same instrument, totally different music. The Huckabays say that music is a part of them. Always a hobby, never a profession, they are not happy unless they are doing some music.

Their interest in music identifies them both as people who are always learning and as people who are always serving. On the one hand they are always seeking to improve their skills; on the other hand they are always open to opportunities to minister with their music.

When it comes to music, they will try anything. As a child, Jim studied violin. Celia took piano lessons. In college Jim joined an evangelistic team, the Christian

Cowboys, where he played hymns on his violin. After a year the leader needed another guitar player, so Jim took up guitar. Celia joined the team after being persuaded to take accordion lessons. Married and on their way to the mission field, they began to sing together. Wherever they went they found that music was an entrance into people's hearts.

Now in their seventies, they are still learning and still serving with their music. Upon moving to Tucson they began attending a large church with a "senior choir" and an orchestra. They both sang in the choir and Jim showed up with his violin at orchestra practice. Facing the challenge of difficult music—some classical, some modern—he perfected his playing as never before.

At the same time he and Celia began attending the local country jam sessions. He practiced fiddling techniques and she became proficient on the harmonica. Ultimately their country connections began to open up opportunities. Rarely does a month go by that they do not provide music for a small church, a Sunday school get-together, a banquet, or a rest home. The music opens doors for further opportunities to minister.

Recently one of their friends became activity director

We trust that seniors would be in a church and involved there. It seems like the seniors have so many opportunities for volunteering: ushering, greeting, stuffing bulletins, parking attendants, shuttle drivers, information booth duty, missions.

JIM AND CELIA HUCKABAY

for a local apartment complex with a large senior population. She invited the Huckabays to put on a program for a St. Patrick's Day potluck dinner that would follow a "Happy Hour." They accepted.

They arrived to a mixed crowd with some a bit happier than others. When they stood to begin the program, Jim stared into the face of a man with a bottle of Jack Daniel's and a bottle of soda water sitting in front of him. Undaunted, the Huckabays presented their usual program, beginning with a few vintage "sing-along songs" accompanied by guitar and accordion. After leading in "When Irish Eyes Are Smiling," Jim played a favorite fiddle tune, "The Irish Washer Woman." Next came a western segment that included a skit about a cowboy going to church. Afterward they sang "At the End of the Trail," a song with a western sound that has heaven in it.

Still playing her "skit character" Celia turned to Jim and suggested, "You're a cowboy and you like to go to church. We should do more church music." They sang "Amazing Grace" and another song or two, then closed with one last sing-along, this time a Christian song. They always use "Burdens Are Lifted at Calvary" for this spot because the tune is easy, the words are repetitive, and the people are likely to remember it even if they're hearing it for the first time.

The Huckabays have repeated this format in many places, including several mobile-home parks. "That's kind of our ministry," Jim explains, "to use a sing-along format and lead up to a gospel conclusion."

When not doing music, the Huckabays are greatly involved in other areas of their church. He teaches two adult classes every Sunday; she is on a rotating teaching roster for kindergarten children. Every Saturday they are among twelve volunteers who stuff three thousand bulletins. Jim is quick to explain that most of the volunteer work in their church is done by seniors. Being part of that workforce continues to give the Huckabays a real sense of purpose in their post-retirement years.

SPOTLIGHT
The Golden Boys

When eight aging men dressed in dark pants, white shirts, and bolo ties make their way to the platform of the Verde Baptist Church in Cottonwood, Arizona, the congregation knows that they are about to hear another rendition by the Golden Boys. The average age of this perpetually smiling group is seventy-three. (The youngest is fifty-seven; the oldest eighty-one.) Two admit to hearing problems. No one denies that age takes its toll on the voice. Still, what they lack in perfection they compensate for with well-chosen music sung from the heart.

Clayton Chance is credited with the initial dream that older voices could still join together in song. He recruited a group of "slightly past prime" singers, and they went to work. One man's dream became eight men's commitment. After four years of weekly one-hour practices the group has graduated from "small Sunday-night crowd" performances to periodic appearances before the five hundred-plus Sunday-morning crowd. They are also making their music known in the greater

Verde Valley, often being asked to sing at dinners in Cottonwood or neighboring towns.

They came from varied backgrounds (farmer, apartment manager, career service, university professor, corporation executive) but they shared a common love for singing. All had sung in church choirs, half had been soloists, seven had sung in quartets, and one had sung in a mixed trio. Five had been song leaders, two had directed choirs, and six had sung in community choruses or college chapel choirs.

Asked what the greatest thing is about being a Golden Boy, they all agree that it is therapeutic, it's a ministry, and it gives them a sense of purpose. Fifty-seven-year-old George added, "I like being the youngest."

For anyone wishing to start a group of "slightly past their prime" singers, the Golden Boys say, "Strike out. Step forward. Ask God for guidance and health." They always open and close their practice sessions with prayer. On the last practice before a performance they may pray for a little extra help. With prayer, hard practice, and a generous dose of enthusiasm, the Golden Boys go forth once more and sing from their hearts.

CHAPTER 29

✦Reassignment: From College Students to Street Kids

*B*ETTIE ELWOOD reluctantly entered the shelter for street children, wondering what she would find in this unfamiliar place. One look at the homeless children with their head lice and broken zippers prompted a bit of self-examination. "How can I do this?" she asked herself. Forcing herself to look into the eyes of the children, she decided that somehow she had to see her situation through their eyes. What would these little children of the Philippines expect of her? What would they want her to do as a white American missionary?

She knew what she wanted to do. She wanted to go back to Silliman University across town, where she and her husband, Doug, had taught intermittently for eighteen years under the Presbyterian Church (USA) board. But for the persuasiveness of a fellow missionary, she wouldn't have come to the shelter at all. She had resisted her colleague's pleas to help him at the shelter because she strongly believed that her calling was to teach at the college level. Only after much persuasion did she consent to teach a Sunday school class at the shelter. Now that she had come, she questioned whether she had made the right decision.

Today, twenty-one years later, Bettie admits that in

SAGE ADVICE

✦✦✦✦✦

Do what you do best, and do it for a worthy cause. Realize that we are called to be Christ's stewards for a whole lifetime. If upon retirement you are blessed with good health, do not let yourself be drawn into the stereotype of retirees who live to be pampered and entertained. We regard this as a terrible waste of the gifts God has given each of us. To resist this temptation may require a new sense of calling, for, after all, a Christian should never retire from the Great Commission.

BETTIE AND DOUG ELWOOD

spite of its bumpy beginning, the initial contact with the children overcame all her questions and any possible hurdles. From that day on her life has been tightly wound with homeless children in the Philippines.

Now seventy-two, Bettie is president and CEO of Little Children of the World, a not-for-profit interdenominational Christian service agency the Elwoods founded to help children at risk. She works twelve hours a day at the agency's headquarters in Etowah, Tennessee, and travels to the Philippines once or twice a year. Douglas, aged seventy-seven and suffering from myasthenia gravis, works six hours a day in his capacity as international director in charge of volunteers and publications. Neither receives any remuneration for their work.

As the Elwoods continue to expand and enlarge their ministry, Bettie admits that her work with the children became a lasting passion from which she has no plans to retire. But the history of their work is an extreme example of "man making plans and God directing steps." By any measuring stick, Doug and Bettie Elwood were unlikely candidates for a ministry devoted to street children. He holds a Ph.D. degree from Edinburg and has written a dozen books, including a definitive work on Jonathan Edwards, *The Philosophy of Jonathan Edwards*. Bettie attended Cornell, then earned her Ph.D. from the University of Manila. Well received in academic circles, they assumed they would teach at the university level for the duration of their stay in the Philippines. But clearly God had other plans, and the Elwoods would be the first to say that in the divine job market there is no such thing as "overqualified" applicants.

After her initial contact with the street children, Bettie worked at the shelter while continuing to teach at Silliman. But even in the classroom she shifted her focus to the children, using an intern program at the university to further the work of the shelter. She sent psychology interns out to look for the street children. After a few years, she gave up her teaching so she could work full-time with the shelter.

Douglas continued teaching at the university until his mandatory retirement by the Presbyterian board, but he worked with Bettie at the shelter on the side. After his teaching years ended, Douglas quickly moved into a greater involvement with the children. He maintains that servants of the Lord need to be open to a new sense of calling in their senior years. "We should be stewards for a lifetime, not just two-thirds of our life," Doug says.

The original shelter out of which Doug and Bettie formed their independent mission was a residential facility funded by various organizations, including World Vision, at different times. While still in the Philippines the Elwoods observed that in most cases there was actually someone who could care for the homeless children—a grandmother or perhaps a sickly mother—if he or she had help. This discovery became foundational to the stated purpose of their mission: to empower community people to take care of the children.

In addition to Little Children of the World, the Elwoods organized a "daughter" mission, based in the Philippines, which they named Little Children of the Philippines (LCP).

The overall program of this multilayered mission seeks to meet both practical and spiritual needs for families at risk. One of the goals of the mission is to introduce the children to Christ and help them become mature Christian disciples. Through the help of the mission, hundreds of children have emerged from poverty. More than forty are now in college with scholarship assistance from the mission's sponsorship program.

As leaders of the two agencies they founded, Doug and Bettie remain heavily involved with the street children of the Philippines. They have no plans to retire. Nor does Bettie have any regrets over leaving a classroom full of college students for a shelter full of street kids.

Contacts:

Little Children of the World, Inc.
361 County Road #475
Etowah, TN 37331
(423) 263-2303
Fax: (423) 263-2303
www.littlechildren.org
E-mail: lcotw@conc.tds.net

Volunteers are needed for overseas and for the U.S. headquarters in Tennessee. Ask for "voluntary service opportunities" brochure.

CHAPTER **30**

✦On Any Given Sunday

*M*ARRIED sixty-one years, Pat and Kathryne Williams still live independently in their three-bedroom brick home near Longview, Texas. Out of the city limits but close to town, the house sits on an acre and a half of land dotted with pin oak, sweet gum, pine, and maple trees. Summers, when the grass grows high, eighty-four-year-old Pat is often found on his riding mower taking care of their grounds. Sundays he and Kathryne regularly attend the early service of their church, but they are less active than they once were. It's not that they have retired from church work—they have taken on new responsibilities.

On any given Sunday the Williamses may be found conducting a worship service in the dining room of a nearby nursing home. Pat leads the singing. Kathryne always reads a poem or some inspirational writing.

Pat explains that he and Kathryne serve "full-time" with the nursing home, meaning they are responsible for the service every Sunday. In addition, they participate twice a month in an evening sing at the home. They work with the hospital chaplain to plan and execute the services at the three hundred-bed nursing home. Many of the forty to fifty patients who fill the room sit in their wheelchairs. Others sit at the tables.

SAGE ADVICE

✦✦✦✦✦

We would advise older seniors to continue in church work, especially with the elderly, doing visitation in homes and hospitals.

PAT AND KATHRYNE WILLIAMS

With four years at their current nursing home and three years at a previous one, Pat and Kathryne have completed seven years in nursing-home ministry. Kathryne's mother spent the last two years of her life in the home where the Williamses now minister. At the time of her death they were holding weekly services at the home. After her death, patients expressed their concern to the Williamses about the continuity of the services. "You're not going to stop coming now, are you?" They didn't.

In his earlier years, Pat worked five days a week for Montgomery Ward, where he was manager of the truck tire sales division. After raising a family, Kathryne worked as a saleslady in a women's dress shop. Much of their time outside working hours was given to their church. "We always worked together," Pat says. They taught Sunday school, worked in music, helped with building projects—whatever was needed.

When counting their blessings, the Williamses place high on the list the neighbors they have enjoyed for nearly forty years. "We all bought large parcels in what was to be a new development," Pat explains. But only five families bought into the development and none has ever left. Pat is quick to point out that for thirty-eight years they have kept their house up-to-date and in good repair. Reaching his eighth decade has not changed that.

In addition to their nursing-home ministry, the Williamses still find time and energy to do visitation in

homes and in the hospital. After sixty-one years of serving together, Pat and Kathryne see no reason to stop now.
On any given Sunday they will be in the early service at
their church. As soon as the pastor says "Amen," they will
be out the door and on their way to the nursing home.

CHAPTER **31**

✦Assignment: China

AT age sixty-four, Dave Crane intended to devote his last year with the mission board under which he had served for thirty-four years to a writing project. His goal was to write the history of the mission in Trinidad where he and his wife, Elaine, had helped establish nineteen churches, a Bible school, and a thirty-acre Christian camp. Instead, he went to Hong Kong for a year and stayed for eight.

Of that experience, Dave says, "I shudder to think that I came within a whisker of missing the icing on the cake of all our years of missionary service if I hadn't gone to Hong Kong."

Dave was born in China of missionary parents and first saw the United States at age nine. Nevertheless, when the mission director asked the Cranes to spend a year in Hong Kong to provide some "maturity" alongside a young couple learning the language, Dave said no.

He didn't want to take on the challenge of relearning the Chinese language that he had all but forgotten in a fifty-five-year absence.

He felt he was too old to help open another mission field.

He had an assignment to write the history of the Trini-

SAGE ADVICE

◆◆◆◆

Make yourself available. Your previous profession can be used in many foreign fields on a short-term or part-time basis. Investigate, ask your pastor, check the mission boards. There is a desperate need for English teachers in China, especially older ones. There are many, many opportunities for older citizens to be useful in the Lord's service. Take time to ask various groups. Don't stop at one; chat with several.

DAVE CRANE

dad mission, and that's where his heart was at the moment.

Still, he felt guilty about saying no, so he suggested that he and Elaine take three months to pray about the possibility. For three months he sought God's leading. None came. Sometimes at night he stared into the darkness and prayed that God would write "Hong Kong" on the wall. He didn't.

At the end of three months he went back to his director and said, "You tell me what to do." The board sent the Cranes to Hong Kong for a year. Eight and a half years later Dave says, "It wasn't Hong Kong only that God wanted; it was China."

From their Hong Kong base, Dave and Elaine began to make trips into China to the area where Dave grew up. Slowly, miraculously, God opened doors. Eventually, with permission from the government, the Cranes moved into China and began to reopen churches that had been closed for forty and fifty years. Dave refers to a letter from the government of China giving him permission to preach and observes, "Only God could do that."

After moving to mainland China, the Cranes located an old mission church in which Dave's father had preached. For years the building had been used as a fertilizer plant. Dave and Elaine were given permission to renovate that building as well as another one in a nearby town.

A year ago the Cranes were in China for the ground-breaking of a church. Originally planned as a renovation project, it will actually be a major building project. Some adjacent property became available, allowing them to build a church to accommodate five hundred. At the government officials' insistence, they will place a large flashing cross on top of the steeple.

Now seventy-five, Dave and his wife go into China every year for at least three months to help reopen churches. They also continue to travel and speak in churches in the U.S. and Canada, sharing the challenge of open doors and talking about what God is doing in China today.

"China is a large country," Dave tells anyone who will listen. "Anything you hear and read about China is true . . . somewhere. There is much persecution, but there are openings."

In spite of their focus on China, Dave never gave up his idea of writing the history of the Trinidad mission. Recently they returned to the island at the invitation of the Christian leadership to "challenge the churches towards faithfulness to the Word of God and missions . . . and to see if something could be put down on paper to tell what God has done in Trinidad."

Meanwhile the story of what God is doing with the Cranes is still unfolding. They no longer talk about "retirement" plans. In fact, when they are finished in Trinidad, they are going back to China to assist in reopening yet another church.

CHAPTER **32**

✦A Mother's Gift

CROSS the front of her garage, spelled out in large wooden letters, is the playful name that Merle Platz and her late husband chose for their Cottonwood, Arizona, home: "Casa Costa Plenty."

At eighty, Merle lives alone and continues an independent lifestyle that has marked her since childhood. "The hardest thing about being alone is getting used to it," Merle observes. The need to take care of herself was hardly a problem. "I was a latchkey kid," she explains. "I had a sick mother who was frequently in a sanitarium and a hardworking father who was never there when I came home from school." She was left to take care of herself.

Still independent, Merle travels alone, frequently making an eight-hour drive to her son's home in southern California. Admittedly she has to watch herself a little more than she did when she was young, but she loves driving and loves the freedom that it gives her.

Her other passion is music. She plays both piano and organ in a variety of settings outside her home. Inside the Casa Costa Plenty, she plays for herself. She finds music therapeutic and recalls that when her husband was ill in the hospital, she would come home and play. After he was gone, she played "a lot."

She remembers with some humor that she didn't want to learn the piano. In fact, she cried when her mother bought the piano and announced that Merle would learn to play. She wanted to play the violin, an instrument that she still loves but never learned to play. Today she looks back with appreciation for the gift of her mother's persistence.

Merle still tries to practice a little every day. She generously volunteers her time in several local retirement homes. Every Sunday afternoon she plays a half hour of hymns and vintage popular pieces at one home. She also plays one Monday a month at the same place. Several Monday nights each month find her at another nursing home.

Merle is the evening pianist at her church, trading off periodically with one other pianist. She fills a key position at her church as accompanist for the Golden Boys, an ensemble made up of senior men. (See spotlight, page 121.) Every Friday morning she practices with the Golden Boys, then hurries away to teach a Bible study.

Currently she is teaching two separate Bible study groups each week. Using the book of Acts at both places, she prepares her own lesson material. A student of the Word throughout her life, Merle is self-taught and depends heavily on material from such greats as Dr. J. Vernon McGee and Dr. Harry Ironside.

She still finds time to volunteer at the hospital for three hours every Wednesday.

Then there's the attention to physical needs. She proclaims that she is in good health and that she makes an effort to get proper rest and exercise. After lunch she often watches reruns of *Bonanza*, then lies down on the floor with a couple pillows for a fifteen-minute nap.

Merle has two children, one in southern California and one in Washington. They have given her seven grand-children, nine great-grandchildren, and one great-great-grandchild. She rotates holidays with the two families and often sees her son between times because he lives closer. While her family occasionally applies pressure on her to move closer, she continues to resist.

"I love my family," she emphasizes, "but I have had to be independent all my life." She doesn't see any need to change that just because she has reached the big *eighty*.

CHAPTER **33**

✦A New Design for
an Old Discipline

*I*N the dining room of their Nashville home,
Charles and Carolyn Oakes eat their meals from an octag-
onal table finished with eighty pieces of inlaid walnut
veneer. The table and the four matching chairs are but a
few of many items created by Charles. He admits that
genes play a heavy part in his woodworking talent since
his grandfather, the first of the family to come to America, was a woodworker who graduated from the Institute
of Fine Arts in Budapest. Charles began his lifelong
hobby out of necessity when, right out of grad school, he
needed to supplement a sparse income. Woodworking
became but one of many entrepreneurial ventures. As
Charles describes it, the Oakes have always been entrepreneurs.

The spirit of entrepreneuring combined with academic
training and an early introduction to discipling others has
prepared Charles for his current passion: mentoring others.

As a fifteen-year-old, Charles sat at the feet of Dawson
Trotman, founder of the Navigators. Charles describes that
period of his life as a time when he discipled other young
men after being "adopted and trained" by a local chapter of
the Navigators. He continued a discipling ministry to new
(and not-so-new) Christians while in the military and

✦✦✦✦✦

***The* critical issue in mentoring is to mentor each person according to his or her God-given purpose. Part of mentoring should be to resurrect and reestablish a sense of purpose in older adults.**

CHARLES AND
CAROLYN OAKES

while attending the University of California at Berkeley, where he worked with InterVarsity, Campus Crusade, and Youth for Christ.

Through those collective experiences he observed that discipling focused primarily on learning doctrine, obeying biblical authority, and developing character. Gradually Charles became aware of a gap in the standard approach. There seemed to be little or no effort to determine God's unique purpose in the life of the individual being discipled; therefore there was no effort to help him or her discover how to fulfill that purpose. He determined to find a new approach.

Now, at age seventy, Charles manages a mentoring program at the seven thousand-member Christ Church of Nashville, Tennessee. His first responsibility after coming to the church was to design and develop the mentor training program, which he now manages.

He teaches that a willingness to mentor each person according to his or her God-given purpose is essential to the mentoring program. The program is focused on high impact/low maintenance men and women, and it attempts to bring them into a higher level of maturity and purpose-driven lifestyle both in the church and in the secular marketplace.

"I love the church," Charles says, "but I have an incessant commitment to a very broad range of secular settings where I want mature believers to have an influence."

By the time he came to Christ Church, he had spent five decades mentoring in the secular world, in churches, and in parachurch organizations. "I have always mentored," he says. "It was a natural thing for me to do. I mentored men to the position of elder in their churches, mentored young professors in the art of teaching and tendering students, and mentored employees to positions for which they were uniquely gifted."

He also mentored his two sons before, at the appropriate time, encouraging them to find new mentors who were more capable to guide them in their chosen careers.

Currently Charles and his wife, Carolyn, are team-mentoring a young couple. Among others, Charles is mentoring a business professional and an ex-pastor of thirty years. He continues to mentor fifteen of the mentors he has trained. Since 1998 he has trained over three hundred mentors, fifty of whom are at Christ Church. They in turn are assisting about four hundred other church members to reach personal growth goals. But, Charles is quick to point out, the influence doesn't stop there. Since the four hundred are in the marketplace, Charles has determined that several thousand people are affected daily by the mentoring program.

Charles has also spent forty years in the field of gerontology, which encompasses a broad array of academic specialists trained in the science of older adults. Convinced that older adults are the most underused resource in the institutional church, he seeks to involve seniors in his mentoring program. He describes today's older adults as counterparts to the Old Testament older adults who contributed to the stability and continuity of the culture, transmitting values and character and skills to the younger.

Purpose is the common thread that runs through both the mentoring program and the work with senior adults. "I have presented to many audiences on the concept of purpose," he says. He notes that afterward, whether the audience is secular or religious, the older adults are the ones who frequently approach him. The question is always the same. "Is it true? Is there still purposeful life for me? You see, I have had this dream that never died and I was wondering . . ." This response has given Charles Oakes a personal mission: to resurrect and reestablish a sense of purpose in older adults.

CHAPTER **34**

✦Just Say "Yes"

*A*T the four thousand-plus member Casas
Adobes Church in Tucson, Arizona, gray-haired parking-
lot attendants assist visitors with directions. The patio
area is lined with tables where elderly women hand out
information on the various ministries of the church.
Today the Jubilee Choir (restricted to singers fifty-five
and older) will sing at the morning service. During the
Sunday school hour, someone who is starting a new
ministry will make the rounds of the senior adult classes
to recruit volunteers. Senior adults are everywhere in this
church—getting the job done, whatever that job may be.

Paul Warren, in his late sixties himself, directs one of
the church ministries that depends solely on senior volunteers. But Paul admits that he was a reluctant volunteer.
He recalls that the Lord spoke to him about this ministry
for some time before he took the plunge. After a career as
a nurseryman, he worked in real estate management with
a friend. While keeping a string of apartments in good
repair, he conceived the idea of providing free service to
people in need. But like Moses, he hesitated. "Why me?"
he asked as he thought about his lack of education and
his questionable abilities. Still, the vision would not go
away. One Saturday morning in a Promise Keepers

SAGE ADVICE

I **think most people are like I was, like when God approached Moses. They think, "Who am I that I should go? I'm nobody special. I'm not highly educated. There are so many other people much more educated than I." But if people will get through that they will realize that the Lord can use anyone. If you feel the call to do something, get involved with something. There is plenty out there to do.**

PAUL WARREN

meeting at the church, he confided to his small group that he was struggling with an idea but was reluctant to pursue it. A friend leaned over, put his hand on Paul's shoulder, and said, "Paul, if God is calling you to do it, why don't you just say yes and do it?"

He did.

Today, as head of the Neighborly Love Ministry, Paul seeks to help single moms and elderly people with housing needs—general maintenance, including exterior and interior repair, and heavy housecleaning. He uses senior volunteers both for their expertise and their availability. Younger adults are generally only available on weekends, but with seniors, Paul can work during the week and, like everyone else, have his weekends free.

Paul's wife, Charlene, admits that this was not the way she visualized their senior years. She sees her basic contribution to the ministry as a willingness to go along with Paul's dream. But she also spends a good many hours on the telephone in connection with the ministry.

As a compromise, Paul agreed to restrict the work to three days a week. One day a week the Warrens volunteer at a local Christian radio station, a task they have done for nearly a dozen years. Charlene notes that they have been with the station longer than any other volunteers. One day a week Paul and Charlene reserve for each other, and weekends are free for Saturday chores and church on Sunday.

In order to start the Neighborly Love Ministry, Paul approached the church's minister to seniors for advice. Soon they had a board of directors, a vision statement, a purpose statement, and a group of volunteers to do the work. Specifically identified as a senior adult program providing home-maintenance care to qualified recipients, they purpose to provide necessary skills to maintain the living quarters of qualified people in the Casas community. Their goals are simple: to accumulate and maintain a pool of maintenance labor, to identify people who need help, and to match the labor resources with the need.

While needy seniors are a target group for the service, the bulk of the work is done for single moms. Paul explains this by the fact that seniors often have more resources, family to help, or money to hire work done. His collection of thank-you notes reminds him that young or old, people appreciate the service.

He explains how he determines which jobs to take on. After a call for assistance comes in, Paul looks the job over. If it's a large involvement of labor and material, he consults with the pastor to seniors. In some cases the two men make a follow-up visit to the site, then discuss it further. At times Paul also turns to the church benevolence committee for guidance. "They have a way of finding out the real need," he says, "and they will give me guidance. If the people want something done that isn't really necessary—it will benefit them but it doesn't need to be done—we don't do it. That's not what we are about."

The work is financed through donations to a special fund in the church. Paul draws on this for cases where the people cannot afford to pay for materials. He also has had good success with local businessmen who donate materials from time to time for the ongoing work.

While affirming that volunteering has been a great blessing to him, Paul admits that there are still times when he asks himself, "Why did I get into this?" There is little time to debate the question. Tomorrow he has five men coming out to reshingle a roof.

On his worst days he is still glad that the vision never went away and that, in spite of his reservations, he decided to just say yes.

SPOTLIGHT

Finding God Faithful

With two careers and eighty years behind him, Moses was not necessarily looking for a third career that morning on the back side of the desert. He was more concerned about finding something for his sheep to eat. (Make that his father-in-law's sheep. Moses didn't really own any sheep.) When confronted with the possibility of leaving the sheep behind to go on a mission for God, Moses said no. Actually, the word no isn't in the text, but Moses gave a lot of reasons why he should refuse the mission.

"Who am I for this job?"

"What if they ask about my credentials?"

"What if no one listens?"

"I'm not a good public speaker."

"Can't you find somebody else?"

Moses was neither the first nor the last reluctant volunteer. He leaves this great example for everyone who senses God is calling him or her to do the difficult or the impossible. In spite of all his questions and doubts, Moses obeyed God. He went on the mission. He took on his third career—as a military leader to lead the Israelites to the Promised Land. In the process he became a mentor to Joshua, his divinely appointed successor. He preached to the people. He wrote songs and he wrote down the law from beginning to end. When he was discouraged (which was often) he talked to God about it and then kept going.

Forty years later he preached his last sermon (the book of Deuteronomy), in which he testified to the faithfulness of God: "His work is perfect." " There is none like Him." Powerful words from one who reluctantly obeyed and allowed God to do the rest!

CHAPTER **35**

✦ Speaking to God,
Writing to Friends
and Family

*E*IGHTY-NINE-year-old Bessie Cole has lived
for twenty years at the Broadway Towers in Knoxville,
Tennessee, which she describes as "a lovely building."
A committed Christian of many years, Bessie has always
served the Lord as she could. Physically limited by the
time she moved to the Towers, she readjusted her goals
and began a ministry of encouragement through cards and
letters.

Her calendar is filled with the birthdays and anniversa-
ries of family, friends, and former students from the academy where she served as dietitian for a number of years.
Her family, to whom she is affectionately known as
Nanny, never wonders what to get Bessie for her own
birthday. She loves receiving boxes of cards, stationery,
and postage stamps.

Along with her letter writing, Bessie continues a lifelong ministry of prayer. To those who know her best,
Bessie is known as an intimate conversationalist with
God. She consistently lifts each member of her family to
the Lord and pleads with Him to meet specific needs in
their lives.

One look at Nanny's family reveals ample evidence
that she is passing on a legacy of faith to succeeding

generations. She has five ordained ministers in her immediate family: a son, a son-in-law, a grandson, and two grandsons-in-law. Many of her children, grandchildren, and great-grandchildren are active in their respective churches. All of them know that no matter where they are, back at Broadway Towers, Nanny is talking to God about their needs.

Her cheerful but weak voice belies the fact that she has lived a hard life. Six children kept her at home working as a full-time mother. Widowed in her late forties, she was forced to find work outside the home, first as a dessert chef at a local high school, then as dietitian at what is now King's Academy. After nearly a dozen years she made a career change and spent the rest of her working years in caregiving situations. Sometimes the elderly. Sometimes motherless grandchildren. Cooking, cleaning, and nursing occupied her days, but even then she was known as the family's designated intercessor.

Hard work and the passing of years have eroded Bessie's body but not her spirit. Determined to do what she can so long as she has breath, she meets each new limitation by readjusting.

Bessie admits that a recent stroke has hampered her writing. So once again she is working her way around a new obstacle. Unable to attend church services, she sends in her tithe every week. Somewhat hampered in her writing, she still sends cards as she can. And she prays.

If the day comes when Bessie can no longer write, she

can still talk to God about her vast network of friends and family. When you have a lifelong prayer ministry, there is always something to do until you draw your last breath.

CHAPTER **36**
✦ Ten-Minute Tapes

*E*LLEN SINGLETON'S husband, Bert, worked
for World Vision for thirteen years, traveling around the
world to help rescue Vietnamese boat people. Although
Ellen was allowed to join him periodically, the Singletons
experienced long periods of separation. Finding a need to
bring balance to her life, Ellen looked for a ministry of her
own. She found her niche in a Scripture tape ministry for
hospitals. Now a widow at sixty-nine, Ellen emphasizes,
"It's not something from which you retire."

Nor is it something from which you move away. The
Singletons relocated twice after Ellen entered into the
tape ministry, and each time she found new hospitals in
which to distribute the tapes.

Ellen credits "a big, tall German" doctor at Harbor
General Hospital in Carson, California, with starting the
hospital tape ministry. He wanted his patients to have the
option of listening to Scripture. Some twenty volunteers,
including Ellen, took the ten-minute tapes around to
various patients.

Later, when the Singletons moved to Glendora, Ellen
asked if she could repeat the ministry at the Foothill Presbyterian Hospital. By this time, she had tapes in English,
Spanish, and Chinese, all made at Azusa Pacific

SAGE ADVICE

✦✦✦✦✦

God gave you your talents. I've always gone by the theory that things you like to do, that's what the Lord likes you to do too.

ELLEN SINGLETON

University. The hospital chaplain welcomed the ministry and introduced Ellen to chaplains from other hospitals. Soon she was distributing tapes to eight different hospitals.

The Singletons began training people who helped distribute the tapes, and in time a chaplain suggested to them that they needed to incorporate the ministry.

Bert came to me at World Vision and said, "Dr. Ted, this idea is working. Would World Vision give us a matching grant to help incorporate it?" We did, and someone at World Vision helped them draw up a logo.

Ellen Singleton explains the ministry as something that just snowballed because it meets needs for people facing all sorts of things: cancer, surgery, even death. "The doctor can say something to them and cheer them up, but the Word of God is living and active and powerful. When God speaks to these people and says, 'I'm not going to leave you or forsake you,' that's all they need to hear."

When Bert finished his years at World Vision, the Singletons began looking for a new balance in their lives. They felt the need to move somewhere where they could concentrate on each other, so they relocated to a small town in central Arizona. Landscaping the new property, meeting new friends, becoming a part of a new church, and entertaining visiting grandchildren occupied much of their time. But the desire to volunteer lingered and the Singletons set aside a "volunteer day" each week. While Bert gave time to the local library, Ellen began knocking at doors to begin another hospital tape ministry.

Currently she has a roster of volunteers who work with her in the ever-expanding ministry. She describes the tape ministry as a brief thing but a powerful thing. "We look upon ourselves as feet and hands, knowing that God will direct us to those who need to hear. We don't have to know whether God is convicting them, comforting them, or what He's doing. It's His Word and all we have to do is be faithful."

In widowhood Ellen continues to be faithful, living her life with this "feet and hands" attitude that is so common among senior volunteers. In addition to overseeing the local tape ministry, she has recently made a trip to Honduras with her surgeon brother. He has been to Honduras several times with a medical team. This year a last-minute replacement was needed because a nurse had major surgery and couldn't go.

"It was too late to replace her," Ellen says, "so they essentially settled for a gofer. I have no medical skills."

With her brother's encouragement she went along and did a variety of things to free up the nurses and doctors: assisted in the pharmacy, managed crowd control, directed patients to the right doctor, and saw that every team member drank a glass of Gatorade every two hours. The medical team examined over a thousand people and filled over four thousand prescriptions.

At home after the short-term missions trip, Ellen declared, "I'd do it again in a moment. When I came home I thought, 'Oh, you did it; you can do it again and again and again.'" But characteristically, still conscious of the need for God-directed balance to her life, she questions whether that is what God will direct her to do. She will wait and see. Meantime, she plans to spend time with her grandchildren and time at the hospital handing out ten-minute tapes.

CHAPTER 37

✦ View from an Albanian Balcony

*V*IRGINIA WIDMAN stood on the balcony of her apartment and watched the crowd gathering in the street below. Thinking it was a Muslim celebration of some kind, she grabbed her camera and began to record "life in Albania." Oblivious to potential danger, she shot picture after picture while the people intermittently waved and shook their fists. The next day she learned that it had been a riot group and that they had broken all the windows in a nearby government building and set it on fire.

A schoolteacher by profession, Virginia went to Albania in the fall of 1996 to teach the children of two missionary couples. She taught four subjects to three eighth-grade girls. While Virginia taught in English, her students also took classes taught by Portuguese- and Albanian-speaking teachers. Amazed at their ability to study in three separate languages, Virginia later had cause to be thankful that the girls were semiproficient in Albanian, a language which she understood not at all.

Things were beginning to get ugly in Albania the spring of 1997. The failed pyramid scheme initiated by the government had turned the people against Albanian officials. Virginia, unable to understand the televised news reports, had no idea what was going on. Little by

SAGE ADVICE

❖❖❖❖❖

This is a time in your life when you have so much to offer, and there's nothing else that's important for eternity except what you do for the Lord. You don't have to go overseas. There are many opportunities to serve the Lord.

VIRGINIA WIDMAN

little, as the girls came for their lessons, she learned the details of the political upheaval that rocked the country.

Public schools shut down. Libraries closed. Public gatherings of more than four were forbidden. Because Virginia had only three students, they continued to meet regularly.

To further complicate the situation, the parents of one of her pupils returned to the States because of illness, and Virginia assumed much of the responsibility for caring for the girl. One night the mother called from the States and told Virginia to get their daughter out of Albania immediately before the borders closed. Still unaware of the magnitude of the problem, Virginia agreed to do whatever the parents advised. Along with the other missionary family she managed to get through to Greece before the borders closed.

In Greece she finished out the school year for the two children who stayed behind. The following spring, with things still unsettled in Albania, she was persuaded to return to Greece to finish another school term.

Today, three years later, Virginia continues to make herself available if needed for other teaching posts with missionary kids. (Prior to Albania, she taught in Argentina.) Meanwhile, another project frequently takes her outside the country. When her church decided to adopt an unreached people group, they recruited Virginia to get a committee together to find an appropriate group. Making the choice became easier when the committee learned that a woman from the church had been appointed to work with the Sindhi people, an unreached group. The church agreed to adopt the Sindhi people as their area of concern, and very soon Virginia was off to London.

In London she attended a meeting of "everyone who was adopting the Sindhi people." Representatives from churches in the U.S., England, and other parts of the world joined with a handful of Sindhi Christians to brainstorm and pray.

"I've never been to a meeting like that," Virginia says. "It was constant. We never went sightseeing. We didn't have the afternoons off. We just met and prayed all morning and all afternoon."

The purpose of the London meeting was to discuss how to organize, how to be most effective in prayer, and how to find ways to reach out to the Sindhi people who are scattered all over the world. When the conferees divided into groups, Virginia joined a half-dozen people who were asked to concentrate on prayer and promotion. As an example of promotion, she says that the group was instrumental in naming the second Sunday of October "International Sindhi Sunday."

Virginia candidly admits that in order to meet with her fellow subcommittee members from various parts of the world, she was forced to learn new ways of communication. E-mail and computer language were as foreign to her as the Albanian language had been, but she became proficient enough to hold electronic committee conferences. Later, her subcommittee initiated a monthly prayer guide that originates with a team member in London, goes to a second member in New York for editing, and ends up with Virginia in Sacramento, who sends it out by e-mail to some one hundred people.

At a follow-up conference in Singapore, conferees gathered for another round of prayer and discussion following much the same format they had used in London. Feeling the need for at least one more brainstorming/prayer session, the group plans to meet in Jakarta next year. When not on the road, Virginia hosts a First Friday prayer meeting in her home for the Sindhi people.

At seventy-two, Virginia loves her version of the retirement years. "But I would hate to do nothing," she says. She quotes her father, who was working on the staff of a church when he died at eighty-seven. He shunned retirement and said of retirees, "Just when they have more time to give, they disappear into their motor homes."

Not so with his daughter. When Virginia Widman disappears, she is more likely to be found at a school in Argentina, a prayer service in Singapore, or even on a balcony in Albania.

CHAPTER **38**

✦ Doing the Math

*A*FTER twenty-plus years in the air force and twenty-three years teaching public school, seventy-year-old Charles Leland Hill is fully entrenched in his third career. While many of his senior friends are enjoying leisurely evenings and lazy weekends, Charles is tutoring high school math students. Four evenings a week and every Saturday, a succession of kids needing help with everything from algebra to calculus make their way to the Hill home in a middle-class neighborhood of Austin, Texas.

Charles has converted one of the five bedrooms into an office to accommodate his tutoring. Prominently displayed in the nine-foot-by-twelve-foot room is an attractively framed copy of the Ten Commandments done in Old English lettering. Hill reserves his desk, framed with book-shelves on both sides and above, for his own use. For his students he uses the small fold-down table at the end of the computer armoire. He sits on one side facing the student.

"I've read more math upside down than I have right-side up," he says. "I always roamed the classroom while the students were working on assignments and answered their questions while facing them instead of standing beside them."

Charles has been tutoring for three years, and so far all

his students have graduated on time and gone on to college. When teachers ask him, "What do you do when you tutor students?" he tells them, "Nothing you wouldn't do if you had the time." In fact, as the basis for his sessions, he reviews whatever concepts the students are currently working on in class and observes them as they apply the concepts. He praises their success and provides constructive criticism when they make errors. He voluntarily meets with their teachers every week to discuss progress.

While students pay for the tutoring sessions, Charles receives nothing extra for meeting with the teachers or for attending the many weekend sports events. But he finds a great sense of fulfillment from all the contact with students. He says, "I can honestly say that I have never been more at ease with life's choices or had a better feeling of accomplishment than I do now that my interests lie in one-on-one tutoring and using my life to influence others."

Tutoring also gives him opportunities for witnessing. He emphasizes that he tries to live his life in such a way that others will know he is a believer. His goal is to be a positive role model for the young people he tutors.

Living his life as a positive role model began early for Charles. He grew up in Kentucky, the son of a pastor. At age thirteen he gave his life to Christ. As a teen he taught Sunday school and led music in the youth meetings. In the air force he served in chapel choirs and as a chapel committee member. Still active in his home church, he is also seen as a role model by his family.

Daughter Laura says of her father, "I think the fact that he is still involved in the lives of high school students as a seventy-year-old speaks volumes. . . . I wish there were more seniors still serving through relationships with younger generations. He enjoys . . . getting to know his students beyond geometry, algebra, or calculus problems. It is sad to me to see seniors exclude themselves in environments completely isolated from other walks of life when we could learn so much from all the big or little things they can offer."

Every Wednesday Laura takes her four young children, ages one through five, for a play day with Grandpa Hill. It is the highlight of their week. They enjoy a midmorning play session before lunch, then more play until their 2 P.M. naptime. Grandpa snatches some rest time for himself while the children nap because soon it will be 4:30. And once again Charles Hill and one of his students will do the math.

CHAPTER **39**

✦ The Only Church in Town

WHEN the late May temperatures begin to rise in Tucson, Arizona, Bill and Dot Hutchison load their travel trailer and head for the higher climes of Arizona's White Mountains. Their destination, the mountain town of Greer, boasts an elevation of 8,500 feet. Few people stay in Greer through the extremely cold winter months. The Hutchisons live there from June through the end of September, but strictly speaking, they don't come to Greer for the climate.

Seven years ago Bill became the resident summer pastor at the only church in Greer. Self-taught in the Scriptures with no formal theological education, he remembers his first Sunday in the resort community pulpit. "My knees were shaking and Dot's hands were shaking as she played the piano."

Prior to their first service, held in the dining room of a local restaurant, the Hutchisons distributed flyers and then waited and hoped that someone would come. Twenty-two people came.

Today Greer Chapel is still the only church in town, but the people worship in an old barn redesigned as a meeting hall. At the front of the building is a raised platform backed by a curtain that hides a storage area and to which Dot adds colorful banners each Sunday. Outside, a prominently displayed sandwich board announces meeting times. Meeting at the barn allows both ample seating and ample parking for the sixty to seventy people who now attend on a regular basis.

The Hutchisons clearly love Greer and love what they are doing in Greer, but they admit that they didn't sign on for this job. They volunteered to come to Greer and help set things up for a mission pastor who would preach and whose wife would play the piano. After the first Sunday the mission pastor said, "Well, Bill, I have four churches on this circuit and I'll be preaching somewhere every Sunday, so it's up to you."

In spite of his lack of training, Bill sees his two previous careers as preparation for their current ministry. For thirty-three years he worked for Mt. Bell telephone company. In the early years they were in small towns with small churches, where Bill taught Bible classes and even did some preaching if needed. Later, as he moved into managerial positions, he did public speaking on a regular basis. After he left the telephone company, Bill and Dot built their own real estate business. Through ten years in the business, both became accustomed to meeting people.

When they sold their business, the Hutchisons planned to spend every summer doing volunteer work in a different location. They went to Greer, thinking it would be for one summer. But their sense of calling grew as they moved into the ministry at the only church in town.

After their second summer in Greer, Bill and Dot signed on for a summer in Alaska. They worked twelve-hour days at a camp managing the summer volunteer staff, which consisted of six couples from all over the lower forty-eight states. While they have been invited back several times, the Hutchisons find there are energy limitations that come with aging. The Alaska experience helped confirm their calling to Greer, and they have returned to Greer every summer since.

When they went to Greer they were told that "everything closes down after Labor Day," so they closed down too. But one year as they left, they saw most of the congregation standing by the road and waving good-bye. It occurred to the Hutchisons that they should not be the first to leave. Since then they have stayed through the end of September.

They learned as they went along that ministry in a summer resort area doesn't fit the traditional mold. Their two-hour Sunday morning meeting includes a time of fellowship. They have no children's ministry because there are no resident children, only occasional visitors. Bill and Dot found other less traditional ways to reach out.

Every Monday morning Bill meets a dozen or more people at 8:00 A.M. and takes them on an all-day hike—a formidable challenge since the hike begins at 8,500 feet and leads on to even higher elevations.

On Wednesday at 7 A.M. there is a men's prayer break-

> ## SAGE ADVICE
> ◆◆◆◆◆
> **There is a tremendous waste of talent in this country. And along with all the talent that's not being used, there is a lot of excitement being missed.**

fast for which Dot cooks. Later there is a women's Bible
study in an RV park.

Thursdays they drive to nearby Springerville, where
they visit an eighty-year-old woman who lives alone. Dot
plays games with her while Bill takes care of yardwork and
other maintenance jobs. One year the Hutchisons painted
the woman's house.

Bill spends Friday mornings preparing for Sunday.
Friday afternoons they play games with about a dozen
people at one of the church member's cabins.

Now in the midst of their seventh summer, the
Hutchisons look over the best congregation in town
and agree that, so long as they are able, Greer is the only
place to be.

CHAPTER 40

✦Making Their
Dream a Reality

*P*AUL AND EDITH WINTER peered over the rim
of the canyon through the windshield of their truck. The
road to the bottom looked to be a formidable journey to
make with a fifth wheeler. She looked at him. He looked at
her. "We're going down there?" They had been so anxious
to hit the road that Paul, an electrician, had taken early
retirement from his job with Clemson University. Now
they wondered whether they should have asked a few more
questions a whole lot earlier. But it was too late to turn
back. Paul shoved the truck into low gear and headed
down the road.

Floydada, here we come!

Floydada, Texas, and the camp at the bottom of the
canyon was the Winters' first assignment with Roving
Volunteers In Christ's Service (RVICS). It was also the
first time anyone from the organization had attempted the
trip to Floydada. Not only did Paul and Edith make it in
good order, they had a great time. Since then they have
traveled from Canada to Mexico, from the East Coast to
Arizona, seeing much of the country, meeting new
friends, and donating their labor to needy Christian
camps, churches, and schools.

To serve with RVICS was something Paul and Edith

First of all, you want to be compatible as husband and wife. And you both should agree that you want to do this. All the couples here are committed together and that's why it works. If one doesn't like it and the other does, it will be a terrible strain.

PAUL AND EDITH WINTER

had dreamed about for twenty years. Their interest in the organization began in New York state at Sacandaga Bible Conference, where they saw a group of Roving Volunteers in action. As Paul and Edith watched the group work together, they decided that when they got older that's what they would like to do. The idea never left them.

During Paul's last years at Clemson University, he and Edith began to research more thoroughly the possibility of following their dream to become part of the RVICS. They prayed regularly that the dream would one day become a reality. They read *The Traveler*, the quarterly magazine of the organization. They visited sites where they knew a group of RVICS would be working. They did a lot of camping with their RV, so they knew what they were getting into.

Paul left Clemson at age sixty-two. He retired in April. They sold their home and bought a fifth wheeler, and by October they were on the road. Among their fellow travelers, they are known as the "rookies" because they are younger than most. Many couples who join the group are in their seventies, and some are eighty. At a recent assignment, the group celebrated the fiftieth wedding anniversary of one of the couples.

There is no such thing as a typical assignment, because each job is different, but the RVICS do follow a routine schedule wherever they go. They do volunteer work four days a week and have three days off. Recently the Winters spent four weeks at Rainbow Acres in Camp Verde, Arizona. At this home for mentally challenged adults, five RVICS couples assisted in a major remodeling project. Paul did electrical work while others repaired roofs and put up drywall.

The women were no less busy in their non-construction-type assignments. Residents of the home, called "ranchers," work at different crafts, some of which are sold in their gift shop. RVICS women assisted in the gift shop as well as the ceramics shop. Edith worked in the rug room stripping blue jeans for the "ranchers" to weave into rugs. She trimmed and packaged Campbell's Soup labels. She spent one morning recycling old tractor-fed computer paper—separating it into single sheets and removing the tractor feed from the edges. "They call it mundane work," she said, "but it doesn't bother me."

On the fifth day, a free day, the group customarily tours area attractions. Tourist attractions in the Camp Verde area include Montezuma Castle cliff dwellings, the ghost town of Jerome, and Sedona's red rock country. For a special dinner out one night, the group went to The Blazing M, a popular chuck wagon–style restaurant with a dinner show featuring "Sons of the Pioneers" style music.

In addition to four work days and three personal days, the schedule for any given project always calls for a weekly group Bible study and a game night. On Sundays each couple is expected to be in church somewhere in the area.

The theme song for the RVICS is "Family of God," and Paul and Edith find that very appropriate. They have gained an extended family through their work with RVICS. On one of their projects the Winters connected with a couple with whom they became fast friends. Now serving in different areas, the two couples keep in touch via e-mail and are making plans to camp together on vacation in Alaska this year.

Paul and Edith find that e-mail is crucial for keeping in touch with family as well. They make every effort to maintain contact with their two daughters and two grandchildren. They send cards from all over the U.S. In addition they have a cell phone that covers the country with no roaming charges and no long-distance charges.

The RVICS ministry is described as an opportunity for Christian couples to travel while doing the Lord's work; to sightsee and relax together and to share their Christian experiences with one another. It is a place to form lasting friendships.

As much as the Winters love their senior lifestyle, they admit that it's not for everyone. They said, "We had camped a lot. We had an RV. We knew what we were getting into." Edith cautions that people should have an idea of what this lifestyle feels like before making a commitment. Speaking for both of them, she adds, "We plan to do this so long as we have the strength."

Contacts:

RVICS International Headquarters
1800 S.E. 4th Street
Smithville, TX 78957
(512) 237-2446
(800) 727-8914
Fax: (512) 237-5119
Office hours: Central Time, Monday through Friday
9 A.M.–12 P.M.
1 P.M.– 4 P.M.

CHAPTER **41**

✦Deliberate Plans, Divine Revisions

*J*AMES AND FAYE BRALEY always knew they needed to plan ahead to follow their dream. What they didn't realize is to what lengths their dream would carry them. They dreamed of being financially independent so they could do consulting with small Christian schools throughout the United States. Their dream led them to a worldwide consulting ministry supported in part by two churches and a number of friends.

Nine years ago Jim began to make plans for a big career change. He had spent his life working with Christian schools doing everything from teaching, to administration, to writing and editing curriculum, to working at the headquarters of the Association for Christian Schools International (ACSI). At age fifty-nine he began to think about becoming a full-time consultant for Christian schools. But he observed that the smaller schools that most needed the service could not afford normal consulting fees. The Braleys needed a plan that would enable Jim to consult for reduced fees or even for no remuneration.

They made a big decision. They sold their southern California home and, for less than half the money, relocated to another community. By investing the rest they realized a monthly income that supplemented the

Look for short-term ministries. In most countries age is revered. Older people in our churches have such vitality left. I encourage you to funnel it into some kind of ministry.

JAMES AND FAYE BRALEY

stipends Jim earned as consultant. For a time, the plan seemed to work.

The picture began to change when ACSI asked Jim to go to Germany to do some workshops at a Christian school. Later he was asked to go to Romania to teach Christian schoolteachers. That 1991 trip proved to be a career-changing one. During the Romania meetings, two ministers of education from Russia came down by train from Moscow and met with Jim. They asked if he would come to Russia and teach schoolteachers how to teach the Bible in the public schools. "I told them I didn't know how to teach atheists how to teach the Bible and they said, 'Well, come and teach them how to become Christians.'" In November of that year Faye and Jim flew to Russia. Suddenly their dream had taken a different turn, and the Braleys have been consulting around the world ever since.

This year alone took them to Russia, the Ukraine, and the Philippines. August frequently finds Jim in France, and every June he teaches in Pennsylvania. When Faye goes along on overseas trips she works in distribution of materials and as a general gofer. Mostly she assists Jim with whatever needs arise.

The expansion of the consulting business necessitated a change in their support arrangement. Because in most cases the Braleys must pay their own airfares plus other expenses, they now have two churches and a few individuals who contribute to the consulting ministry through a fund set up with ACSI.

Now in their late sixties, Jim and Faye adamantly reject the idea of retirement ("It's not a biblical concept"), but they admit that with age come health challenges. Jim has had one bout with a blood clot brought on by a long overseas flight. For the next year he curtailed lengthy trips while his doctor carefully monitored his condition. Now on long flights he takes along a special pad that allows him to exercise his legs while sitting in his seat. Whenever possible, he breaks up a flight so that he can walk between legs of the journey. As an added precaution he seldom travels without Faye these days. They take it one trip at a time, knowing that if Jim has another blood clot they may have to give up long-distance traveling.

Like many of their peers, the Braleys have an aged mother to care for. For five years while Jim's mother lived with them, Faye remained at home to care for her mother-in-law. At present she is in a nursing home but there are many arrangements that have to be made whenever the Braleys go overseas.

"We have to arrange for any contingencies because it wouldn't be easy for us to get back," Jim explains. "It's always a burden to make sure we have given all the information necessary so people can act independently of us in case we can't get back." While others might choose to stay home under such circumstances, the Braleys believe that if God opens the door and provides for them to minister, he will provide for Jim's mom while she is here without them. "It's hard to do that," Jim admits. But for now they believe that God wants them to follow their dream.

CHAPTER **42**

◆Turning Seventy-Five in a Strange Land

*A*RDETH FRISBEY wondered what awaited her as the plane began to circle for a landing in Budapest. Below her the Danube River flowed between the two parts of the city, Buda and Pest. Somewhere on the Pest side a building was being renovated as a center for ACSI (Association of Christian Schools International). Ardeth had come to Hungary to serve as secretary for the center. On the flight over, with neither cake nor candles, she had turned sixty-seven.

She never dreamed that she would spend eight more birthdays in this beautiful place where patience and ingenuity proved to be as essential as office skills.

Ardeth's first week at the center coincided with the final week of renovation done by a team from the U.S. During that chaotic week she helped with shopping, cooking, washing dishes, doing laundry, and even making beds. When workers uncovered a bathtub in one of the basement rooms they cleaned and refurbished the room for Ardeth. Next to it, in what had apparently been a small office, they created a 12 by 18 foot living space for her. This became her home while in Hungary.

When the team left, Ardeth was free to concentrate on setting up the office. "Can you imagine establishing an

SAGE ADVICE
✦✦✦✦✦

If seniors can maintain good health, that is an important asset. But even if one's health is not so good, a positive attitude toward helping others is also very important.

ARDETH FRISBEY

office in a large city like Budapest with no telephone or fax service available?" she asks. "It made for a very interesting first year." Across town, another ACSI couple lived in a section that had telephone service, so they had the center's telephone and fax service in their home. To receive messages, Ardeth called them every day from a public telephone four blocks from the center. During winter, she bundled up and plodded through the snow. Summer or winter, she often stood in line as others used the telephone.

When not trudging back and forth to the telephone, Ardeth set up files, established her legal status within the country, became a signatory for ACSI for banking purposes and official documents, and took care of mail.

If receiving telephone messages was complicated, taking care of mail and legal documents was no less so. Several days a week Ardeth walked to the post office, where every piece of mail was individually weighed. After postage was affixed and canceled by hand, she received a receipt for office mail and paid for the transaction. Taking care of legal status meant going to the immigration division of the national government and waiting in long lines for several hours until an officer was available. To further complicate the process, Ardeth had no knowledge of the language, so she was forced to wait for an English-speaking officer.

Ardeth regards her position as a signatory for banking

duties as one of the most important tasks she performed in Budapest. She handled all the banking and the cash boxes in the office. She kept strict account of U.S. funds and Hungarian funds and submitted monthly reports to the ACSI International ministries office. In time she was promoted to office manager, a title that didn't change her duties but did describe more accurately what she had been doing all along.

In addition to an incredible amount of patience, Ardeth brought to the task a background that prepared her for working with foreign governments. For twenty-seven years Ardeth worked at the Pennsylvania State University Office of International Students. Working on the nonacademic part of admission for the international students, she handled all their immigration work and gave counsel and a listening ear as needed. While there, she and her husband were involved with a graduate group of InterVarsity students who invited internationals to their activities.

Prior to her years at Pennsylvania State, Ardeth spent a number of years at Michigan State University, first as a student, then as an employee while her husband did graduate work. At MSU she met many international students and did typing for them. Later she accompanied her husband when his company sent him to Iran for three years.

It had been her husband's dream to spend their retirement years traveling to various mission fields serving the missionaries in specific ways. When he died before retirement age, Ardeth had to revise her plans. She continued to work for a time while she determined what she should do as a widow. A contact from friends who had been graduate students at Pennsylvania led her to Hungary. They asked her, "What are you doing for the next year?"

That was in 1993.

In August of 2001, Ardeth celebrated another birthday in the midst of final preparations to return to the U.S. As she turned seventy-five in a strange land, she described herself as "one of God's willing servants whom He has given a great opportunity to serve while enjoying life in the process."

SPOTLIGHT
Where Is He Now?

For over fifty years the deep, resonating voice of George Beverly Shea has been heard around the world in connection with the crusades of Billy Graham. For the same span of time his song "I'd Rather Have Jesus" has continued to be a favorite choice of soloists everywhere.

The story of "I'd Rather Have Jesus" is almost as familiar as the song. Shea was twenty-three when his mother placed a poem by Rhea H. Miller on the piano, and that very evening he composed the music for the now world-famous song.

At ninety-two it would seem natural that Shea would "take a breather," at least from the strenuous routine of concerts. But in a recent interview with Bonnie Shepherd of *Lifewise* magazine, Shea confirmed that he's "still packing his bag" for the Billy Graham city missions and for concert dates in near and far-off places.

Where is he now? Perhaps at home in Montreat, North Carolina, but definitely not retired. Perhaps he is even now on the road again. While he is best remembered for his long connection with the Graham crusades, for his compositions, and for his deep bass voice, he told Shepherd, "I hope people will remember the simplicity of the songs, the thought-provoking messages, and that I stayed on pitch."

From that thought one might extract a message for all senior soloists: Old soloists never quit; they lift their voices in song at every opportunity so they can keep telling "the old, old story of Jesus and his love."

CHAPTER **43**

✦From the End of the World to the Ends of the Earth

WHERE would a seventy-year-old man and his sixty-something wife go to reach over nine million people a year with the Word of God? A teeming marketplace in the heart of a mega-metropolis comes to mind. An isolated country home at the end of a six-mile stretch of dirt road seems a less likely choice.

The road to the community of Cherry, Arizona (population less than 100), is officially marked "Primitive Road" and is lined with dust-covered mesquite, desert willows, and a few scattered junipers. At the edge of this former gold-mining town sits an unpretentious two-story building where Bud and Betty Miller live. Formerly the main lodge of a privately owned camp, the house has a plywood exterior painted brown. A half dozen smaller cabins are scattered among the trees.

Inside one cabin that serves as their ministry office, Betty opens a closet door and points to a mass of wires. "This is how we do it," she says. From their microscopic community, which is best described as "the end of the world," the Millers operate www.Bible.com, a Web site that reaches to "the ends of the earth."

Obviously, the success of their Web site ministry does not depend upon location. Instead, the Millers emphasize,

*B*e willing to change. See what God has for you. You may think, "God wouldn't want me to do this because of my age," but it might be the exact thing God wants you to do. If so, He will empower you to do it.

BUD AND BETTY MILLER

its success has hinged upon the couple's willingness to adapt to new methods of ministering to a world in need.

The confessed "computer illiterates" were introduced to the possibilities of the Web site through a piece of junk mail. While sorting their mail one day, Betty ran across a flyer that extolled the Internet as the "next great marketing frontier." The Millers, who had been in various kinds of ministry for years, were at a crossroads, wondering what God would have them do in the future. They decided to investigate the Internet.

When they contacted the man behind the junk-mail flyer, they discovered he was a believer. From there things began to develop. With the man's help, the Millers set up a Web site, but for the first year they did nothing with it.

They set about learning the language and trying to see how Web sites worked. Bud describes their early steps as wobbly. Little by little they found people who could tutor them, give technical advice, and help them understand how to add information to their Web site. Eventually Betty became the on-site technician, a fact which Bud describes as "scary."

Today they offer a correspondence course on their Web site, as well as an online magazine. The King James

Version of the Bible can be accessed in sixty different languages. They also have commentaries where ministers or serious Bible students can go to find what they need in their own language.

Their software allows them to trace the origin of every hit to their Web site. Last year they received in excess of nine million visits from one hundred different countries, with a significant number coming from countries where Christianity is not allowed. In the privacy of their homes people from Saudi Arabia, Kuwait, Qatar, and the United Arab Emirates are seeking to know more about the Bible. The ever-expanding ministry now registers over 800,000 visits a month and receives 600 e-mails every day.

No one is more amazed at the success of www.Bible.com than the Millers. Betty describes their biggest challenge as accepting the fact that God has thrust them into this ministry. With no previous computer experience, they describe themselves as most unlikely candidates. They see their main contribution to the process as "just obeying God."

To assist them in the work, the Millers have three full-time secretaries who live on the grounds in the cabins surrounding the main house. One takes care of e-mail, one runs the online bookstore, and one is the financial secretary.

While the Millers are hard-pressed to explain the most exciting thing about the ministry, they often point to a young man from China whom they had the privilege of winning to Christ. Later they mailed the new believer a Bible in his own language, which he subsequently shared with a friend. Today the two are "holding church" together in a town where there is no fellowship of believers. The Millers find the entire ministry so exciting that they can't wait from one day to the next to see what will happen.

They plan to continue the ministry so long as they have the strength. Bud says, "I never think about the fact that in twenty years I'll be in my nineties. It's just not part of the equation. I believe that God will empower us to finish our work."

By any standard, the Millers are an unlikely couple living in an unlikely place, reaching millions of people with the Word. But they are also living examples of what seniors can do when they are willing to meet new challenges, continue to learn, and continue to work hard.

"We're both working harder than we've ever worked," Bud declares. "I wouldn't do this for anyone but the Lord."

CHAPTER **44**

✦ Finishing Well

*I*N his letter to the church at Philippi, the apostle Paul wrote, "being confident of this, that he who began a good work in you will carry it on to completion until the day of Christ Jesus" (Philippians 1:6).

Since God wants to complete His work in us until we draw our last breath, it is important for us to utilize our giftedness, our talents, and energy in "works of righteousness" that bring glory to Him. As you have seen through the stories in this book, this can be done no matter what our state in life may be.

In the previous chapters we highlighted men, women, and couples who in their senior years have offered their lives to the Lord and in doing so discovered how productive these years can be. I believe that heaven will be filled with people who have more stories of what they did after age seventy than anything they did before.

Many years ago at Christmastime, General William Booth, the founder of the Salvation Army, decided to send a special holiday greeting to his key officers around the world. He composed a sentence that he wanted to telegraph to each of them, but he found the cost prohibitive. He cut the sentence in half and still it was far too expensive. Finally he sent a greeting of just one word: "Others."

His colleagues understood the message immediately— they were ministers in Christ's name to others who needed assistance, help, and the message of hope.

That is the message of this book. Each of us can minister to others in various ways using our experience, our hours, and our talents on their behalf.

After sixty-plus years of active leadership responsibilities in Christian ministry, I wondered what God would have for me in my remaining days. I had enjoyed serving in key executive roles in a large Christian publishing house, heading up an international youth ministry, and serving as chief executive officer of World Vision, the large international relief and development ministry. I soon learned that I could use my experiences in consulting with young Christian leaders. My calendar rapidly filled up with consulting engagements for a host of ministries across the nation. In addition, I was able to use my experience by serving on the boards of a significant number of Christian institutions—colleges, missions, and service agencies.

I join with friends listed in this book in giving praise to God for the privilege of having, in this "fourth career," the joy of continual and meaningful involvement even as an octogenarian. Facing the "post-retirement" years is not about getting old. It's about life. In fact, I've found it to be the most wonderful season of life.

As a young Christian I received from God my life verse, which is found in Psalm 32:8: "I will instruct you and teach you in the way you should go; I will guide you with My eye" (NKJV). This promise has been abundantly fulfilled over all these years and continues to this day in my retirement experience. May it be so for you as well.

While preparing this last chapter, I received a letter from a very dear former colleague of mine in which he writes, "We have such a bright future ahead of us. If the veil could be lifted for a moment and we could see behind the curtain of heaven, I'm sure we could not contain our excitement and overwhelming sense of wonder at what our extravagantly generous Lord has been preparing."

What a wonderful prospect this is for all of us who love and serve the Savior. May we continue to serve Him until we go charging into heaven. At our journey's end, may we hear Him say, "Well done, good and faithful servant."

POSTSCRIPT

*"It's not too late. I'm in the last inning.
But a lot of ball games have been won
in the last inning."*

from a sermon by the Reverend Peter Lord,
Park Avenue Baptist Church, Titusville, Florida, 1991

ABOUT THE AUTHOR

An executive with finely honed skills and diverse interests, **Ted W. Engstrom** is a highly respected leader within
the Christian community and in management circles.

As the former president and chief executive officer of
World Vision and a director on numerous boards, including Focus on the Family, Engstrom is one of today's most
influential leaders in American religion and social
service. Before joining World Vision, he was president of
Youth for Christ International for six years. He also
served as interim president at Azusa Pacific University.
He has been awarded five honorary degrees.

A prolific editor and author, Engstrom has written
more than fifty books and hundreds of magazine articles.
He is the author of the best-seller *The Making of a Christian Leader*, and coauthor of the best-selling *Managing
Your Time*. Other books by Engstrom include *Reflections
on a Pilgrimage: Six Decades of Service*, *The Pursuit of Excel-
lence*, *Motivation to Last a Lifetime*, and *Integrity*.

As president emeritus of World Vision, Ted Engstrom
continues to maintain a full schedule of speaking, writing,
and leadership training engagements.

FOCUS ON THE FAMILY®
Welcome to the *Family!*

Whether you received this book as a gift, borrowed it from a friend, or purchased it yourself, we're glad you read it! It's just one of the many helpful, insightful, and encouraging resources produced by Focus on the Family.

In fact, that's what Focus on the Family is all about—providing inspiration, information, and biblically based advice to people in all stages of life.

It began in 1977 with the vision of one man, Dr. James Dobson, a licensed psychologist and author of 16 best-selling books on marriage, parenting, and family. Alarmed by the societal, political, and economic pressures that were threatening the existence of the American family, Dr. Dobson founded Focus on the Family with one employee—an assistant— and a once-a-week radio broadcast, aired on only 36 stations.

Now an international organization, Focus on the Family is dedicated to preserving Judeo-Christian values and strengthening the family through more than 70 different ministries, including eight separate daily radio broadcasts; television public service announcements; 10 publications; and a steady series of books and award-winning films and videos for people of all ages and interests.

Recognizing the needs of, as well as the sacrifices and important contributions made by, such diverse groups as educators, physicians, attorneys, crisis pregnancy center staff, and single parents, Focus on the Family offers specific outreaches to uphold and minister to these individuals, too. And it's all done for one purpose, and one purpose only: to encourage and strengthen individuals and families through the life-changing message of Jesus Christ.

• • •

For more information about the ministry, or if we can be of help to your family, simply write to Focus on the Family, Colorado Springs, CO 80995 or call 1-800-A-FAMILY (1-800-232-6459). Friends in Canada may write Focus on the Family, P.O. Box 9800, Stn. Terminal, Vancouver, B.C. V6B 4G3 or call 1-800-661-9800. Visit our Web site—www.family.org— to learn more about Focus on the Family or to find out if there is an associate office in your country.

We'd love to hear from you!

Adding Life to Your Years
From Focus on the Family ®

LifeWise Magazine
Celebrate midlife and beyond with Focus on the Family's *LifeWise.* This publication encourages spiritual growth, intergenerational relationships and positive involvement in the culture. Each bi-monthly issue includes inspirational stories, practical ideas and relevant topics.

The Gift of Grandparenting
shows grandparents how to take an active role in creating strong spiritual and emotional family ties through activities emphasizing fun and faith. Whether the grandchildren live around the corner or around the country, this book gives every grandparent new ways to enjoy the marvelous gift of grandparenting.

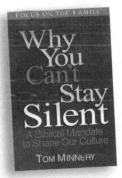

Why You Can't Stay Silent
By Tom Minnery
Throughout history, courageous Christians have stood for righteousness and changed the world. Tom Minnery, head of Focus on the Family's public policy division, makes a compelling case for Christian involvement in the important issues of our day. Learn how to be an effective witness and an involved citizen in a culture that desperately needs to hear the truth spoken with love.

• • •

Look for these special books in your Christian bookstore or request a copy by calling 1-800-A-FAMILY (1-800-232-6459). Friends in Canada may write Focus on the Family, P.O. Box 9800, Stn. Terminal, Vancouver, B.C. V6B 4G3 or call 1-800-661-9800.

Visit our Web site (www.family.org) to learn more about the ministry or find out if there is a Focus on the Family office in your country.